About the Author

David Bale served in the RAF for nearly thirty years, and was stationed in the Canal Zone, Singapore, Germany, the Persian Gulf and Labuan. He has worked in local government in Oxford and Wales, is a British Legion welfare caseworker, and now lives in Exmouth, Devon.

RAF LABUAN BORNEO

David Bale

With Best Wishes
David Bale

Book Guild Publishing

Sussex, England

First published in Great Britain in 2014 by
The Book Guild Ltd
The Werks
45 Church Road
Hove, BN3 2BE

Typesetting in Garamond by
YHT Ltd, London

Printed and bound in Great Britain by
CPI Group (UK) Ltd, Croydon, CR0 4YY

A catalogue record for this book is available from
The British Library.

ISBN 978 1 909716 04 9

This book is dedicated to my late brother, Bernard Bale, Master Navigator RAF and later with Swissair.

My eternal thanks to my dear wife Phyll for her forbearance and proof reading.

Thanks, too, to the editorial, design and production staff at Book Guild Publishing.

Contents

Preface

The gestation of my first book was almost forty years. The thought came to me at Labuan, while thinking of my hometown, that somebody should detail the experiences of the men I knew who had returned from the war during my boyhood.

Not long after that book was published the thought of a story about my time on Labuan occurred to me as I walked home from collecting my pension one sunny morning. This became a larger project, and I was delighted with the responses from various sources following a few advertisements, which led to one or two visits, some interesting phone conversations and many letters, photographs and e-mails.

It also gave me an excuse to make several more visits to The National Archives at Kew. Sad to say Ken Appleford, one of my sources about post war Sunderland times and later the Shackleton search and rescue operation, has since died. He was a fine man and typical of the members of the Kipper Fleet.

I first heard of the island of Labuan from my late brother when he returned in 1948 from his first tour in the Far East, and I was not at all daunted to be told by my OC that I was to be detached there away from my diesel bay duties. Some years earlier I had read Agnes Keith's book *The Land Below the Wind* and found, like many before and since, that the island and the small friendly detachment was an ideal posting. I had played Australians at rugby, but knew few of them until we assisted in the Sabre Ferry. Neither had I known very much about the Japanese occupation or the Australian liberation.

I hope that this short history goes some way to fill in those gaps. The Confrontation was little publicised while I was comfortably enjoying my first tour in Germany, but I was brought up to date when I met my brother when we both returned to UK for a family funeral.

I hope I have done justice to those good men who lost their lives in that forgotten corner of the world.

History

Labuan Island, five degrees north of the equator, lies off the northwest coast of mainland Borneo, formerly British North Borneo, now Sabah. The island's name comes from the Malay word for an anchorage, *labhuan*.

The island was a part of the Majajpahit Empire until the fourteenth century when it was ruled by the Sultan of Brunei, until being ceded to Britain. Captain G.R. Mundy of HMS *Iris* took possession on behalf of Queen Victoria on 24th December 1846. At that time there were no permanent residents apart from resting fishermen. Borneo became a Crown Colony in 1847 with its own governor and officials. In August 1848 Labuan was declared a free port and opened to settlers. Chinese merchants from Singapore opened shops, and vegetable and fruit cultivation started.

Carlos Quarteron, a native of Cadiz, had been a trader sea captain in both legitimate trade and slave running, before studying for the priesthood in Rome at the age of 41. Ordained in 1855, he was made Prefect of North Borneo and in 1857 with four Italian priests started a Catholic mission on Labuan. Left alone in 1860 he had little success and returned to Rome to seek missionary help. In Rome it was arranged that the Prefecture of North Borneo be assigned to the Mill Hill Fathers.

In June 1860 there was an objection in the House of Commons reported in Hansard: 'the idea of sending vessels to Labuan was ridiculous, and trusted the House would not throw money away on a station which was of no earthly use'. Labuan was used as an anti-piracy base. A request for a Royal Commission to enquire into the proceedings of Sir James Brooke, the Governor of Labuan, and Royal Navy operations against the Dyaks and Sakarran of Borneo, when over 500 men were killed, was talked out in the House of Commons.

The island was also used as a coaling station between Singapore and Hong Kong, and later for the submarine cable between those two colonies, the population of Labuan then being about 4000. In 1869 Mr Pope-Hennessy was congratulated in the House of Commons on his entire success in the government of Labuan: 'By his energy and good sense he had been able to develop the coal mines, which were so important to the future prosperity of Labuan.'

It is estimated that half a million tons of coal were mined over the 64 years, mainly by convict labour from Hong Kong. The mine closed in 1911, but the 106-foot chimney and tunnels remain, with a tourist centre attached. The coal was transported by rail along the route of Jalan Tun Mustapha, which for some years had been MacArthur Road.

In 1881 a Royal Charter was granted to the British North Borneo Company led by Mr Alfred Dent, who had pressed for a charter for a few years. He was joined by four further directors. The terms of the charter distinctly stated that the government would have no responsibility for military protection.

Fr Thomas Jackson arrived in 1881 and bought Mr Hugh Low's estate for 620 shillings, intending to build a school and seminary. He found Quarteron's yacht; the ship's bell was still in use up to the time of the Japanese invasion. Jackson reported in 1883 that there was no prospect of mission work, but he needed a base for missionaries to visit the coasts. 'Labuan would also be a most suitable place for a school for natives collected from the various tribes of North Borneo. There is a substantial house, there are about 10 nominal Catholics.' He reported mission work of one infant baptism, and returned to England in 1896. He was succeeded by Fr Pundleider who conducted Mass for the Catholics working in the coal mines. The first White Sisters arrived in Labuan in 1900, and six years later Fr Pundleider returned to Europe. Labuan became a head station for missionary work in 1913 with the arrival of Fr Willems and the number of Catholics increased.

In 1890 British North Borneo was created a British Protectorate, to be administered by The British North Borneo Company whose headquarters were in London. The company employed the Governor and officials of British North Borneo. Labuan was a British Colony administered by a Resident. From 1906 until 1912 Labuan was a part of the settlement of Singapore; in 1912 it was made a Straits Settlement in its own right.

During 1920 HMS *Renown* had been converted to provide accommodation, a cinema, squash court and promenade deck for use as a royal yacht. The Prince of Wales used the ship to tour Australia and New Zealand. During a later tour of India and Japan he visited the island of Labuan from HMS *Renown* in 1922. At this time there was a radio station VCK on Labuan.

In September 1923 a Japanese company asked to acquire land on Labuan for oil storage purposes. The Resident refused permission and referred the matter to the Governor of Straits Settlements, Sir L. Guillemard, who proposed to the Secretary of State for Foreign Affairs that all such future proposals should be refused. During October the Secretary of State, the

Duke of Devonshire, consulted the War Office, Admiralty and Foreign Office regarding this matter, together with an application by Nippon Yussan Ltd to film the port of Singapore. He concurred with the instruction to the Resident that all such future applications should be refused [CO 537/915].

The first church on the existing site was built by Fr Stotter in 1932, who also founded St Anne's School, which in 1934 was handed over to the White Sisters.

Throughout the 1930s an annual resources form was submitted by the Governor to list naval, military and air resources in Borneo, the latter to exclude Royal Air Force (RAF) matters. In 1935 it was agreed that, as no air resources existed, this section need only be completed on a four-yearly basis. It then transpired that there were residents on the mainland with experience of aviation, and the return for 1935 listed the following:

Messrs Oxley   Captain Royal Flying Corps (RFC) 1916–18, CFS Certificate 2185

     Fenton   Royal Naval Air Service/RAF 1917–18, Observer

     Cox   7 hrs De Haviland Moths

     Rutter   1918 Observer, stopped flying due to medical advice

     Chisholm   New Zealand licence issued March 1932

     Dr Stookes R Ae Club Certificate 1843, Instructor 1916–18.

In 1936 Dr Stookes declared an Aeronca Float Seaplane manufactured in June 1936 and used for medical visits to difficult places. He had been gazetted to the Royal Flying Corps from 2nd Dragoons in October 1916 as a Temporary Lt Observer with 14 Squadron, and as a Flight Commander with the Military Cross in February 1917.

Aeronca Float Seaplane. (Photo: Osa & Martin Johnson Museum)

J. Baxter RA, who had flown 119 hours in DH6, BE2, RE8 and the Bristol Fighter, was added to the list. Finally in 1937 a Mr F.H. Wren was added; he had served in RFC from 1917–1919 and had accumulated 300 hours in BE2, RE8, FE2 and the Bristol Fighter [CO 874/378].

The return also detailed radio and communication facilities; the only mention of Labuan was that the Cable Office at Labuan was operated by the Eastern Extension Cable Company. There had been a project to open up air facilities in British Borneo, and aerodrome sites had been selected and surveyed, but as there was no immediate prospect of British aircraft being available to use the aerodromes the project was postponed except the landing ground at Kuching and a landing strip at Miri.

Following liberation by Australian forces there was an interim British Military Administration. On the 15th July 1946 Acting Governor Mr James Calder assumed the government of the new colony of North Borneo and British Military Administration ceased.

Mr E.F. Twining, later Lord Twining, became Governor of the Colony from 1946 until 1949. The Labuan Town Board was set up in 1947 to administer the island. In 1956 Free Port status was reinstated and Labuan was once again a Duty Free port.

The island became part of Sabah following the establishment of Malaysia in 1963. In 1984 Labuan was ceded to the federal government by Sabah and made a federal territory. In 1990 it was declared an international offshore financial centre and free trade zone.

Aerial view of Labuan 1944. (Photo: A.W.M.)

Royal Air Force and Pre-War Defence

The Royal Air Force started building up their presence in the region in February 1928 when the Far East Flight of Supermarine Southampton twin-engine flying boats arrived at Seletar, Singapore. This unit was later redesignated as No 205 Squadron under the command of Squadron Leader G.E. Livock DFC AFC, and embarked on a series of survey flights, known by the flying boat fraternity as 'cruises'.

In July 1930 Sqn Ldr Livock with aircraft S1419 and S1149 undertook the first Borneo Survey Cruise, familiarising and checking on suitable alighting and mooring areas. There were further cruises in May 1931 and October 1934. Vic Wise, writing as *ozleckie* on the RAF Forum, was with 205 Squadron in 1966 when, during the squadron's 50th anniversary celebration, Gp Capt. G.E. Livock DFC AFC RAF (rtd) was the guest of honour and later Reviewing Officer for the parade. Earlier that year a Shackleton on detachment at Labuan had flown over the Spratly Islands, claimed an unnamed triangular reef and named it Livock Reef in his honour: 10° 11′ 38″ N, 115° 17′ 43″ E.

Southampton flying boat. (Photo: RAF Museum Livock collection)

In 1935 205 Squadron re-equipped with the Short Singapore, a larger four-engined flying boat. During March 1938 two aircraft K6910 and K8859 flew to Kuching, Bintulu, Barah River, Labuan, Kudat, Jeeselton, Brunei and Sandakan on a further survey flight. RAF Form 540 Operation Record Book (ORB) lists a further flight by Short Singapore K6917 to Borneo from 4th to 10th October 1940 with landings at Labuan on the 7th and 9th, refuelling by using four-gallon cans from a contractor's lighter, the quickest being recorded at Labuan as 550 gallons in 18 minutes. The last recorded flight to Labuan by a 205 Squadron Singapore was K6918 in February 1941. The Short Singapore remained on squadron strength until October 1941 when they were handed over to the Royal New Zealand Air Force.

During 1941 the squadron re-equipped with the Catalina, the aircrew being ferried to Manila to collect the new aircraft via Borneo by BOAC charter aircraft. On 1st October 1941 the CinC was flown to Labuan and on the 3rd this aircraft flew what must be the first RAF operational flight from Labuan to reconnoitre Itu Aba, the largest of the Spratly Islands which the Japanese had occupied and were developing as a submarine base.

Catalina, Singapore. (Photo: Imperial War Museum)

The Resident was given a reconnaissance flight of the island on the 6th before the aircraft returned to Seletar. On 20th and 21st October further Catalina flights were staged via Labuan to Hong Kong and Manila [AIR 27/ 1214].

230 Squadron RAF also operated Short Singapore flying boats, arriving at Seletar in January 1937. The squadron re-equipped with Short Sunderland in June 1938. The first record of a Sunderland landing at Labuan was L2164 in September 1938 [AIR 27/1422]. 230 Squadron had carried out operations in

the late 1930s according to Guy Warner (*Fly Past* December 2006). Its Short Singapore and Short Sunderland flying boats had transported colonial officers while stationed at Seletar.

Sunderland flying boat. (Photo: Author)

Borneo (then partly Dutch, partly British) occupies a position of great strategic importance. It lies across the main sea routes from the north to Malaya and Sumatra. Strongly held, it could have been one of the main bastions of defence, but neither the Dutch nor the British had the necessary resources to defend it. Available forces had to be concentrated further south for the defence of Singapore and Java, and all that could be spared for Borneo and the outlying islands were small detachments at important points which it was hoped might prove to be a deterrent to attack.

Air Chief Marshal Sir Robert Brooke-Popham, Commander in Chief, Far East, suggested that 200 RAF and Dutch aircraft be used to defend Sarawak, Brunei, Labuan and British North Borneo. Brooke-Popham stated that this should be sufficient to defend the territories against any Japanese attack. His request was declined by the British and Dutch governments, on the grounds that the aircraft were simply not available.

In December 1940 a detachment of 2nd Battalion 15th Punjab Regiment, Indian Army was sent to Kuching, under a Second Lieutenant. The thirty men had a single 15-cwt truck. They were later joined by B Detachment under Major Davis and 2/Lt Temple, 100 men and two 15-cwt trucks. By January 1941 the troops were training for emergency denial of oil refinery facilities. C Company was sent to Lutong where they were engaged in building anti-aircraft posts. In March of 1941 they were joined by the Hong Kong/Singapore gunners. In May the whole battalion arrived in Kuching: five officers, seven Viceroy's commissioned officers (VCOs) and 348 soldiers aboard HMS *Park*, five officers, and seven VCOs and 345 soldiers aboard the *Wu Sue*. The commanding officer was appointed OC Troops Sarawak and Brunei [WO 172/95].

In June a further draft of thirty-six soldiers, two water carriers and two cooks arrived [WO 172/213]. This Indian Army battalion and supporters comprised the sole British unit in Borneo. The battalion has a memorial in the Labuan Commonwealth War Graves Cemetery.

Japanese Occupation

To gain control of the oilfields, and to guard the flank of their advance on Malaya, the Japanese decided, as a subsidiary operation to their Malayan campaign, to seize British Borneo. This operation was launched by the Southern Army eight days after the initial attack on Malaya.

It had been decided by the British that no attempt should be made to defend British North Borneo, Brunei or Labuan. The Governor of North Borneo, Mr Robert Smith, was informed that the volunteers and police were to be used solely for the maintenance of internal security. However, it was decided to defend Kuching because of its airfield and because its occupation by the enemy would give access to the important Dutch airfield at Singkawang.

On 20th November 1941 the Japanese Kawaguchi Brigade was activated under the direct command of the Southern Army: 35th Infantry Brigade commanded by Major-General Kiyotake Kawaguchi, comprising a Brigade Headquarters, 124th Infantry Regiment, with attached engineer, signal and medical units. In ten transport ships, with a cruiser and four-destroyer escort, landings were made at Miri and Seria on 16th December 1941.

Once news of the landings reached Air Headquarters, Far East, a reconnaissance took place and Dutch naval aircraft attacked the moored ships. On 19th December a Dornier Do 24 flying boat (X32) of Marine Luchtvaart Dienst, the Royal Netherlands East Indies Naval Air Service, from Tarakan Island, sank the Japanese destroyer *Shinonome* and another damaged a landing ship.

On 22nd December two Japanese battalions re-embarked to attack Kuching, leaving the other to secure all British Borneo outside Sarawak. On 28th December Major General Kawaguchi ordered Lieutenant Colonel Watanabe to advance on the 31st by landing barges to Brunei with one battalion collecting boats to be used in the attack on North Borneo. The Japanese soldiers of the Watanabe Force discovered that the British had destroyed any ships left in the harbour, so that only small native boats remained.

On 1st January 1942 two infantry platoons led by a company commander

9

Dornier Do 24. (Photo: Dornier)

landed on Labuan Island, capturing the British Resident, Hugh Humphrey, who later recalled, 'I was repeatedly hit by a Japanese officer with his sword (in its scabbard) and exhibited for 24 hours to the public in an improvised cage, on the grounds that, before the Japanese arrived, I had sabotaged the war effort of the Imperial Japanese Forces by destroying stocks of aviation fuel on the island.'

Agnes Keith, the American author who had written about pre-war Borneo in her classic book *The Land Below the Wind* (alas, now out of print) had lived in Borneo since 1934. In 1939 she returned from leave in America when her husband had been ordered to return to his post as Director of Agriculture at Sandakan.

Following the Japanese occupation the Governor of Borneo had initially, in concurrence with Japanese demands, agreed that certain men in essential services should be released from internment in an attempt to work for the good of the civilian population. Shortly afterwards British and Dutch priests, nuns and all civilian officials, with the exception of doctors, were interned. The Tyrolean priests John Unterberger and Mark Obertegger and one Tyrolean nun were not interned, but their movements were much restricted. Father Wachter, who was Austrian by birth but held a North Borneo passport, had served in Borneo since 1905. He was quite fearless in his dealings with the Japanese. Together with the other Tyrolean priests Fr Wachter was executed by the Japanese on 6th August 1945.

Agnes Keith was hospitalised. Writing in *Three Came Home* she said Dr Stookes 'was being interned and externed [sic] every few weeks, at the will of the Japanese. His plane was an inducement to them to keep him outside prison camp.' She did not think anyone else had the temerity to fly it. For

10

Japanese landing, 14 January 1942. (Photo: A.W.M.)

years he had been flying to inaccessible Borneo places, landing on rivers in all kinds of weather, in order to care for the sick. Dr Stookes, a man who had interrupted his medical studies to serve with gallantry in the 1914–1919 war and had devoted years to the care of people in Borneo, together with four other prominent Europeans, was executed by the Japanese on 7th July 1945.

In January 1943 Mrs Keith, together with forty-six other women and fifteen children, travelled on an open ship's deck to a new unknown prison, with no food from Monday to Thursday. They stopped briefly at Jesselton and were allowed ashore at Labuan for a walk on the jetty. Their boat lay

11

Japanese troops marching through Labuan. (Photo: A.W.M.)

alongside a captured Philippine ship with Philippine prisoners below deck; the fate of those prisoners is unknown. Nine days after leaving Sandakan the boat arrived at Kuching where the Keith family remained imprisoned until September 1945.

The Japanese named the island Maida in September 1942, in memory of General Maida who was killed en route to Labuan. An airstrip of 5800 feet in length was built, and the following Japanese Air Army units were recorded as based on Labuan, the 10th Independent Flying Brigade comprising: 83rd Sentai equipped with Mitsubishi Ki-51 two-seater ground attack aircraft, Allied code name (Sonia); a two-seater ground attack aircraft which was suited to operation from rough and short airstrips and used throughout the war. 83rd Sentai also used the Kawasaki Ki-45 two-seater, twin-engine heavy fighters (Nick), which proved effective against the B-24 bomber. The 34th Sentai were equipped with the Kawasaki Ki-48 twin-engine light bomber (Lily); these aircraft had proved effective in China, but were too slow and inadequately armed against Allied fighter aircraft. 89th Dokuritsu-Chutai were equipped with Ki-51 (Sonia) and Tachikawa Ki-54 (Hickory) light transport. One of the latter was taken to Australia following the surrender and is held by the Australian War Memorial in Canberra.

Mitsubishi Ki-51. (Photo: Unknown)

During 1943–45 Japanese positions on Borneo were bombed by Allied air forces from the South West Pacific Area. In February 1942 the American Far East Air Force was re-designated as 5th Army Air Force, and in November 1942 it started action against Japanese forces in New Guinea with a long hard campaign in conjunction with Royal Australian Air Force (RAAF) and Royal New Zealand Air Force (RNZAF) squadrons. The first record I could find concerning Labuan was the loss of a 43 Squadron RAAF Catalina mine-laying aircraft and six aircrew on 21st April 1944.

As the land campaign succeeded, so the air forces moved into advanced bases and the bomber units were able to attack the enemy further afield. By 1944 5th Army Air Force had again become part of the American Far East Air Force. The principal heavy bomber was the Consolidated Aircraft Corporation Liberator, B-24 in American parlance. During 1943 RAAF squadrons started to re-equip with the Liberator. No 24 Squadron first used the aircraft in June 1944; with 21 and 23 Squadrons they formed 82 Bomber Wing RAAF.

The first B-24 raids to strike oil installations at Balikpapaan started in late September 1944 with further raids during October. On 24th October the Sandakan area was attacked by B-24, B-25 and fighter-bomber aircraft and on the 30th Sandakan airfield was attacked by P-38s. By this time B-24 bombers were based at Morotai, Leyte and Noemfoor islands.

During November B-24s with P-38 and P-47 fighters supporting launched a major strike against oil installations at Tarakan; B-24s and B-25s attacked shipping in Brunei Bay on two occasions and armed reconnaissance and strikes were flown against airfield and shipping targets of opportunity. This type of attack continued in early December. On 10th December B-24s attacked Labuan docks and Lutong refinery. Activity intensified towards the end of the year with attacks on oil, shipping and airfield targets.

January 1945 saw more attacks on Miri and Jesselton airfields; during February there were four raids on Labuan airfield by B-24 bombers, followed by another on 1st March. Later in the month fighter-bombers carried out harassing attacks on the Borneo airfields; the attacks on Sandakan, Jesselton and Labuan were said to be devastating.

Labuan airstrip was bombed again by B-24 aircraft on 20th April, and in May P-38 fighters attacked the airfield on the 6th, B-25 bombers attacked on the 8th and on the 12th a joint force of B-24, B-25 and P-38 hit targets on Labuan and in Brunei Bay. A flak ship near Labuan was attacked by P 38 fighters on the 16th.

On 21st May Liberator A72-177 of 200 Flight RAAF captained by Flt Lt K.R.N. Emmett, a unit engaged on special duties for the Allied Intelligence

Bureau, was lost with a crew of eleven airmen and three special operatives. This small unit lost three aircraft in a short period of time in this theatre.

Between the first and ninth of June 1945 there were six days of attacks by B-24, B- 25, P-38 and Beaufighter aircraft on Victoria, Labuan airstrip and supply routes. 30 Squadron RAAF lost a Beaufighter and crew, Fg Off G.S. McKenzie and Sgt W.J. Gilfillan, on the latter date. The following week saw bombing and strafing attacks in support of the Australian 9 Division landings. On 11th June 22 Squadron RAAF, based on Morotai, lost another Beaufighter in operations against Labuan.

Prisoners of War

The fate and history of the hundreds of prisoners of war under the Japanese has been thoroughly researched by Lynette Ramsay Silver in her excellent book *Sandakan, A Conspiracy of Silence*. It is a most moving book and the source, with Commonwealth War Graves details, of much of my information.

> In July 1942 the Japanese proposed drafting 2000 Australian Imperial Force (AIF) troops from Selerang for overseas duty. Given the promise of better facilities and abundant food there were plenty of volunteers, but in the event only 1500 were available, the balance being made up by including convalescents and older men. The latter were included on Japanese assurances that it was to be a "holiday camp". Considering the possibility of a revolt, senior officers compiled a balanced draft of various combat units. These troops were moved to Kuching and Sandakan where they were employed as slave labour on airfield construction. [*Sandakan* page 33]

Captain L.C. Matthews MC of the Australian Corps of Signals was supplied with guns and pistols by the local underground in readiness for a possible uprising; these weapons were secreted outside the PoW camp. He arranged medical supplies and ran a radio news service. He was in contact with the Philippine guerrilla forces and could have escaped. He was arrested and subjected to starvation and torture in an attempt to make him betray his contacts. In March 1944 at Kuching the Japanese executed him. In 1947 he was awarded a posthumous George Cross in recognition of distinguished services while a prisoner of war in Japanese hands. He is buried and commemorated at Labuan.

> In June 1944 a working party of 100 was sent from Sandakan to Labuan to help in the construction of an airfield, which was being built to defend the fleet anchorage off Brunei. Capt Nagai, in charge, with 57 soldiers and 16 guards the prisoners arrived on 16 June and were confined to a compound in the grounds of the Victoria Golf Club, near

the harbour. On 15th August they were joined by a party of 200 from Kuching. [*Sandakan* page 157]

The Japanese built the airstrip, using prisoners of war as labourers; the strip was shorter and at an angle to the post war runway.

Between September and December more than one third of the hundred men from Sandakan had died from malaria and starvation. The compound at Victoria had been bombed so the prisoners were moved to the 3 mile peg, which was where 23yr old Henry Ford, who had volunteered to join the Labuan party in the belief that anywhere would be better than Kuching, died from a combination of malaria and beri beri on 3rd December. [*Sandakan* page 166]

Silver wrote:

The number of PoWs known to be transferred to Labuan is 290; 99 British and one AIF from Sandakan and 185 British and five AIF from Kuching, but who they were is not known. The figures quoted were derived from Japanese statements and recovery records.

In March 1945 the 112 remaining PoWs with fifteen Formosan guards departed to Kuching, went to Brunei, eight weeks after, leaving 37 dead, the 81 known survivors were joined at Kuala Belait by seven Indian soldiers. The number of survivors who made the next move to Miri on 27 May was 51. There followed the instruction from Tokyo – annihilate them all and do not leave any traces.

Of the 300 prisoners who had arrived at Labuan the previous year, not one was left alive. [*Sandakan* page 215]

Silver's book deals with the labyrinthine reasons, political and military, for the failure to attempt rescue of prisoners during the years that many still survived. When a successful rescue was mounted only escapees survived.

Fifty-one bodies of men who died in captivity on the mainland and who were originally buried at Jesselton (now Kota Kinabulu) were recovered from their marked graves by 23 Australian War Graves unit and buried at Labuan War Cemetery. Buried or commemorated at Labuan are almost 100 Australian soldiers who had fought in Malaya and Singapore and had died in captivity from starvation, disease and barbarous treatment. Nearly 600 British soldiers buried at the War Grave Cemetery died or were slain in captivity; fewer than twenty of these were British infantrymen.

There are twenty-three men of the Straits Settlement Volunteer Force, six of the Federal Malay States Volunteer Force, two of the North Borneo Volunteer Force and one each from the Federal Malay State Police, the Malacca Local Defence Force and the Kedah Volunteer Force buried at Labuan, all of whom fought, were captured and died in captivity.

Of the 500 Royal Artillery gunners and attached soldiers buried, fewer than 100 served in Malaya and Singapore before the surrender. 35 Light Anti-aircraft (LAA) regiment and 6 HAA regiment had been destined for Basra in the Middle East, but at Durban they had been transferred to SS *Narkunda* and sent to Singapore, arriving at Keppel Harbour on 13th January 1942 and shortly after going into captivity. 35 LAA regiment have ninety-four men and 6 HAA have fifty men, not including attached troops, buried at Labuan.

Two other artillery regiments, 21 and 48 LAA and attached personnel, had also been destined for Basra and had left UK aboard the *Duchess of Athol*, having Christmas dinner 1941 at Freetown. At Durban they had been transferred to the troopship *Dunera* for the defence of Singapore, but en route Singapore fell and they sailed into Batavia, now Djakarta, and shortly after went into captivity.

There are sixty-five men of 21 LAA and 158 of 48 LAA, again not including attached troops, among the dead at Labuan. All of the above died in captivity under horrifying conditions.

Among the twelve airmen reburied from Jesselton were AC1 J.B. Bradshaw of 84 Squadron; LAC I. Fox, AC1 Hendy, LAC R.H. Morgan and AC1 J.G. Myers of 211 Squadron, two Blenheim units that arrived from the Middle East too late to stem the Japanese advance. AC1 E.F. Chadburn had been a member of 242 Squadron, a Hurricane squadron that had arrived in Singapore in January 1942 after air superiority had been lost, and been dispersed in Java and Sumatra a month later.

The cemetery was visited by Lady Mountbatten in November 1945 and officially opened on 28th December. Over sixty years later the memory of these men is honoured by Malaysian forces and veterans' organisations.

Australian war graves. (Photo: A.W.M.)

Australian war graves. (Photo: A.W.M.)

LABUAN'S WAR CEMETERY . . . .

Australian Graves On Sunlit Jungle Hilltop

On the top of the hill that overlooks Victoria Harbour, Labuan, red Australian roses are growing between the tropic growth of banana palms and elephant grass. Across the flat top of the hill are the graves of 3,904 known and unknown Servicemen.

MORE than seven years have passed since the grey barges came out of the dawn to spill jungle-green soldiers onto the harbour's narrow beach.

These men were Australians, veterans of the long and arduous jungle fighting of New Guinea. But Labuan was most stubbornly defended.

Neither side took prisoners. The Japanese, blasted off the foreshore by the rockets of the supporting craft, were entrenched in depth.

The fighting that followed could rank with the toughest of any Pacific campaign. When it was over the lovely island was soaked in blood.

As in other campaigns in Borneo, there had been no time to bury the dead. They lay in the jungle swamps, and the ugly red and brown hawks circled in the sky.

When the echoes of the Hiroshima bomb sounded peace across the world the Australian soldiers had moved on from Labuan.

The prosperous island was a shambles of wreckage and dumps. Under the fast-growing mat of the jungle were the remains of the dead. The war had been won, but the price had been paid.

By A SPECIAL CORRESPONDENT RECENTLY AT LABUAN

On the top of the hill, two camouflaged buildings survived the violence of war. They were the headquarters of the Ninth Division and the administrative office of the Sixth Australian General Hospital.

To-day, freshly painted and demure in the harsh sunlight, the same buildings stand at the gates of the Imperial War Graves Cemetery.

They are fine gates these, sweeping back from the glaring tarmac of the road in a soft blend of white sandstone and red brick.

These words are newly engraved into the soft stone: "Hereon are recorded the names of officers and men of the British Commonwealth of Nations who died within and around Borneo during the 1939-1945 war and whose graves are known only to God."

Before the year is out, skilled and patient hands will have chiselled 7,000 names into the walls of the gate.

In the shade of a row of gardenia bushes are long rows of graves of which the bronze plaques can say only: "A soldier of the 1939-1945 war known unto God."

Many of them died on the dreadful journey from Sandakan to Ranau, the slow forced march of fevered prisoners of the Japanese which gave new meaning to the old cliche of man's inhumanity to man.

The War Graves team which followed the route from Sandakan, where 2,300 men started to Ranau, where 260 men arrived, found many unidentifiable remains.

Others were found in shallow graves under the hard white sand of the Borneo beaches where the turtles crawl and the monkeys scamper after shrimps under the long shadows of the casuarinas.

Many were found on Labuan itself, on the island of brave bones where so many had been tried and none had been found wanting.

Now they sleep in the green the air is fragrant with gardenia and frangipanni, hibiscus and African tulip, oleander and wild orchid.

Around the cemetery the red roses from Australia, in brilliant bloom, speak for the gardens of home.

Under the timeless blue sky

War cemetery. (Photo: Basil Frost)

Commonwealth war graves. (Photo: B. Roche)

Liberation, 1945

Following the fall of Singapore and the Dutch East Indies, Australia had to consider its own defence and recalled the Australian Army divisions from the Middle East and Spitfire squadrons from England. Defence of Australia would now depend on cooperation with the USA.

The island of Borneo came within the scope of operations of South West Pacific Area (SWPA) under the command of General Douglas MacArthur. Despite its oilfields Borneo did not feature high on MacArthur's list of priorities. He was obsessively determined to re-take the Philippines at all costs, arguing that American occupation would hasten the defeat of Japan. MacArthur saw that his return to the Philippines, which he had left hurriedly in 1942, would restore American prestige and honour. It was an apparent case of political expediency overriding military strategy. The Australian priority was to gain the freedom of prisoners of war held by the Japanese.

The Borneo Campaign of 1945 was the last major Allied campaign in the South West Pacific Area during World War II. In a series of amphibious assaults between 1st May and 21st July the Australian Corps, under General Leslie Morshead, attacked Japanese forces occupying the island. Allied naval and air forces, centred on the US 7th Fleet, the Australian First Tactical Air Force and the US 5th and 13th Air Forces also played important roles in the campaign. 24 Squadron RAAF lost two Liberators, A72-61 and A72-64, and twenty-three aircrew on the 2nd and 5th of July.

They were resisted by Imperial Japanese Navy and Army forces in southern and eastern Borneo under Vice-Admiral Kamada and in the northwest by Lieutenant-General Baba Masao.

Although the campaign was criticised, it did achieve a number of objectives such as increasing the isolation of significant Japanese forces occupying the main part of the Dutch East Indies, capturing major oil supplies and freeing Allied prisoners of war who were being held in deteriorating conditions.

The campaign, mounted from Morotai, opened with a landing on the small island of Tarakan off the northeast coast on 1st May. The Australian forces under 22 Brigade AIF suffered heavy losses, 217 of whom were subsequently buried at Labuan. 2/23, 2/24 and 2/48 Battalions, 2/4 Commando Squadron and 2/2 and 2/3 Pioneer Battalions were supported by C Squadron 2/9 Armoured, 2/2 Machine-gun Battalion and 2/7 Field Artillery Regiment.

Notable among the many Australian dead buried at Labuan is Lieutenant T.C. Derrick VC DCM of 2/48 Bn AIF. He had enlisted in 1940 and served in the Middle East; at Tobruk from April to October 1941 he had been recommended for a Military Medal and promoted to Corporal. At Tel el Eisa on 10th/11th July 1942 he attacked three machine-gun posts, personally capturing 100 prisoners. He was awarded a Distinguished Conduct Medal, and on 28th July was promoted to Sergeant and returned to Australia with the remainder of the Division in February 1943.

The Division retrained and re-equipped in Australia and embarked for New Guinea. On the Huon peninsula, on 24th November 1943, Derrick's platoon was ordered to attack Sattelberg. Thousands of Japanese were dug in on a mountain and many unsuccessful attempts were made under heavy fire. The task appeared impossible and the Company was ordered to retire. Sergeant Derrick was granted permission to make one last attempt. He personally destroyed one post with hand grenades, and his second section were heavily attacked by machine-guns and grenades from six enemy posts. Without regard for his personal safety he went ahead of the leading men and with grenades so completely demoralised the enemy that they fled. The Company was thus enabled to gain its first foothold on the precipitous ground. On four separate occasions Sergeant Derrick threw grenades at a range of 5 to 7 yards until the remaining three posts were silenced.

Derrick was recommended for the Victoria Cross and, with a commission conceding only on the unusual condition that he be allowed to return to 2/48 Battalion, this was reluctantly agreed. The award of the Victoria Cross was gazetted on 24th April 1945. At Tarakan, during a night counterattack on 22nd May 1945 Derrick was mortally wounded. He continued to inspire his men: when stretcher bearers arrived he insisted other wounded men be taken out first. He died of his wounds on 23rd May 1945.

Earlier, on 12th May 1945 at Tarakan, Corporal John Bernard Mackey VC of 2/3 Pioneer Battalion AIF was in charge of a section which came under fire from three well-sited enemy positions. Corporal Mackey charged the first position and bayoneted the gunner, killing the second crew with grenades. Changing his rifle for a sub machine-gun he attacked the second machine-gun position. He was killed, but not before he had killed two more of the enemy. The award of a Victoria Cross was gazetted in November 1945; he was reburied at the Commonwealth War Grave Cemetery on Labuan.

The Tarakan attack was followed on 1st June by simultaneous assaults on Labuan and the coast of Brunei. This operation became Oboe 6.

T.C. Derrick VC DCM. (Photo: A.W.M.)

Oboe Six

The naval force assembled for the invasion favoured the port of Victoria as providing the best facilities in the area, with three timber wharves and sheltered anchorage for a limited number of cruisers and destroyers.

The Japanese airstrips on Labuan and at Miri had been heavily bombed and were considered non-operational. Japanese naval forces deployed in and around Singapore, comprised four cruisers, two of which were damaged, and four destroyers. It was thought unlikely that they would interfere with operations in the Brunei Bay area. Attacks were considered more likely from suicide boats or submarines. The main danger was from mines, which had been laid by both the Allies and the Japanese; this necessitated extensive minesweeping.

Rear-Admiral Royal RAN was the naval commander in direct command of the operation. General Wooten commanded the landing force of two brigade groups AIF, 20th Brigadier Windeyer and 24th Brigadier Porter. Air Vice Marshal Bostock commanded the Allied Air Forces concerned. The Cruiser Covering Force comprised the American ships *Nashville*, *Phoenix*, *Boise*, HMAS *Hobart* and five destroyers including HMAS *Arunta*, and was commanded by Admiral Berkey.

The Labuan landing was to be on 'Brown Beach', extending from Victoria town to Ramsay Point, a distance of about 1200 yards. The Labuan 'Brown Beach' landing would be on a two-battalion front using US Alligator amphibious vehicles and tanks of 2/9 Armoured Regiment, a troop of Frog flamethrower tanks, a commando squadron, one company from 2/2 Machine-gun Bn, the 2/12 Field Regiment including 4.2-inch mortar assault troops and LAA units, US 727 Amphibious Tractor Bn and the 593rd Engineer Boat and Shore Regiment.

The Minesweeping and Hydrographic Group had a vital task with fifty minesweeping and fire support craft, including HMAS *Lachlan*, USS *YMS160* and USS *Satinleaf*. The complete assault echelon of eighty-five ships which followed included thirty-four landing ship tanks (LST), twenty-two landing craft infantry (LSI), twenty-two landing craft mechanised (LCM) and the Australian landing ships HMAS *Manoora*, HMAS *Kanimbla*, and HMAS *Westralia*.

The first arrival in Brunei Bay at dawn on 7th June was the Minesweeping Group; HMAS *Lachlan* laid channel approach buoys and carried out check soundings of the approaches. On 8th June the cruisers bombarded Muara Island; meanwhile one of *Lachlan*'s boats laid buoys in and near Victoria Harbour.

The Allies suffered the only ship casualty of the operation during the afternoon of 8th June. The minesweeper USS *Salute* struck a mine, buckled amidships and both bow and stern started sinking. Two landing craft attempted to salvage the minesweeper, but they were unable to control her flooding and the ship sank. Lost with the ship and posted as lost at sea were E.F. Banach, W.T. Brown, K.C. Crotwell, R.M. Ojala, R.C. Shafer, C.J. Swanson, W.G. Turley, D.E. Van Dreese and D.C. Lowrey Jr. Thirty-seven men were wounded. The men are listed as 'Missing in Action' at the Manila American Cemetery. (The wreckage of this ship is now one of Labuan's recreational dive sites.)

On 9th June it was learned that the heavy cruiser *Ashigara* had been sunk off Sumatra by HMS *Trenchant*, making Japanese naval intervention even less likely. On the same day Fg Off G.S. McKenzie and Sgt W.J. Gilfillan of 30 Squadron were killed when their Beaufighter A8-156 hit trees and burned following a rocket attack near Beaufort. On the following day Beaufighter A8-177 of 31 Squadron was badly damaged during an attack on Labuan and crashed on return to Sanga Sanga airstrip.

On Sunday 10th June the main body of the Attack Group and 30 landing craft went to Brown Beach: HMAS *Manoora*, USS *Titania* and HMAS *Westralia* were observed to be on station in the transport area. The only immediate enemy reaction was a lone Japanese aircraft, which dropped a bomb that landed between USS *Titania* and an LST and did no damage.

HMAS *Hobart* opened fire with a pre-assault bombardment on Labuan at 8.15 am, firing 549 rounds of 6-inch and 461 of 4-inch shells, joined by Attack Group support craft and aerial bombing. The first wave of assault troops landed at 9.14 am on Brown Beach, which was taken without opposition.

Half an hour before the landings five heavy bomber squadrons, about sixty aircraft, bombed the Japanese defences. The landing went in with 2/43 Bn supported by two troops of the 2/9 Armoured Matildas at 9.20 am; on the coast road they encountered very strong opposition. By 9.45 am the two troops of artillery were ashore, ready for action within thirty minutes, and by late afternoon all twenty guns plus four mortars were deployed. In two days 24 Bty had fired 1205 rounds at one particular target.

On the left flank 2/28 Bn with one troop of tanks landed without mishap and moving aggressively overland captured the wharves and jetties, purposely not bombed, although the enemy resisted stubbornly all day.

Landing ships LSTs 56,128,595. (Photo: Tom Wilson)

Street scene, Victoria. (Photo: Tom Wilson)

Devastation. (Photo: Tom Wilson)

Pre-invasion bomb damage. (Photo: Tom Wilson)

USS *Barcoo* and her convoy of landing craft arrived at Brunei Bay at 12 noon and entered Victoria Harbour. The convoy dispersed to anchorage and Barcoo took up patrol duties.

On shore progress was rapid. At 11 am Brigadier Porter assumed command of his troops ashore at Labuan and a few minutes later General MacArthur, with Admiral Royal, General Morshead and General Kenney, went ashore from USS *Boise*. General MacArthur did not need to get his feet wet on this occasion. Later in the day General Wootten set up headquarters ashore and assumed command.

Gen MacArthur and Lt/Gen Morshead. (Photo: Tom Wilson)

By the end of the day the Australians held the principal airstrip and the main town of Victoria. Unloading was rapid; the three Australian landing ships, USS *Titania* and *Carter Hall*, the five destroyer transports and twenty-four landing craft were all unloaded on that day. On the 11th the larger ships departed, escorted by three destroyers.

At first light 2/28 Bn moved off with Matildas towards Flagstaff Hill, coming under small arms fire. Captain Lushington's company carried the objective where the Union Jack was raised. The right flank of 2/28 Bn came under heavy fire from positions beyond the high ground. The sappers cleared the minefield covered by Matilda tanks and the defence was overcome.

The infantry battalions of 24 Brigade lost sixty men, now buried at Labuan; the total losses of 9 Division in regaining Brunei, Labuan and Sarawak were over 120 men. One casualty was William Smith, a War Correspondent.

The Australian warships *Hobart* and *Arunta* had left Brunei Bay on 12th June but returned with HMS *Shropshire*, recently refitted in Australia, on Sunday 17th June. Rear-Admiral Royal in *Rocky Mount* with Task Group TG.74.3 sailed for Tawitawi and relinquished responsibility for naval gunfire support to *Shropshire*, *Hobart* and *Arunta* and USS *Hart* and *Metcalfe*.

An enemy-held area one mile north of Victoria Harbour and one mile west of the airstrip, known as the Pocket, was the only unsubdued part of the island. *Shropshire* carried out bombardments against these strongpoints on 18th and 19th June. Australian artillery was firing across the airfield construction camp to support attempts to break into the redoubt.

31

On the night of 20th June several Japanese soldiers, many with fused bombs on their backs, broke through from their defensive positions and attempted suicide attacks on the airstrip and wharves; several skirmishes occurred during the night. By morning forty-nine of the enemy had been killed and the remainder captured. On the following day the last pocket of organised resistance was assaulted. Labuan Island was under Australian control.

During July and August 1945, 7 Division AIF attacked Balikpapan losing over 200 men, all of whom are buried at Labuan.

Airfield Construction

The strategic intention was to establish an airfield of 9000 feet on Labuan which would place Hainan Island, part of Thailand, the whole of Malaya and Singapore, all of Java and the northern part of Sumatra within range of Liberator bombers.

This was the task facing the RAAF Airfield Construction Wing, under the command of Gp Capt. W.A. Dale DSO. Sqn Ldr J. Trench commanded 4 Airfield Construction Squadron (ACS); Sqn Ldr J.N. Edwards commanded 5 Airfield Construction Squadron.

Don Northmore, who had been an Airfield Construction Sergeant, recalled in later years:

Early in April 1945, two NCOs of No. 62 Airfield Construction (AC) Wing were sent on special operational duty to Morotai to select camp sites for the Wing and the AC Squadrons where we would stage waiting for the 24th Brigade 9th Division to arrive.

At this time, the Americans were conscious of an imbalance in the Lend-Lease costs and were only allowing commissioned officers to fly on operations in their aircraft and were charging the Australian Government, $40.00 U.S. per head to transport Australian servicemen under Lend-Lease arrangements. Sgt. Northmore and Cpl. Allen were ordered by their Adjutant, to roll up the sleeves of their shirts to hide the rank chevrons and were duly issued with an air travel authority (which still exists) as Flight Lieutenant (Flt Lt) and Pilot Officer (Plt Off) respectively. The surnames were those of officers serving with the Wing.

The two men presented themselves to the U.S. transport officer, resplendent in their grubby faded jungle greens, battered slouch hats, carrying their Thompson guns and gear. While weighing in, they heard the call over the P. A. 'Two Australian Officers', and they were the object of some interest as they walked out to the plane, where groups of immaculately uniformed young officers, direct from the U.S. training schools, looked at them with amazement. It seemed they didn't know Australians were engaged in the war.

On arrival in Morotai, the two NCOs made arrangements for camp sites and the transfer of No. 61 A.C. Wings site and tents to that of 62 A.C. Wing. They also visited No. 14 A.C.S. who were due for relief after completing the construction of Pitoe and Wama strips.

In due course the various formations of army, naval and air force components arrived and set about preparing for the first all Australian combined service actions in Borneo.

No. 4 Airfield Construction Squadron

Silas Edwards, a Flt Lt Building Officer of 4 ACS RAAF, wrote in 1981:

... about our departure from Biak to take part in the landing at Labuan. ... Preparation for the move to Labuan was a well-organised affair. We knew in advance that we were to move on and would require a complete pre-cut camp. We had earlier prepared our pre-cut buildings for the move from Noemfoor to Biak. This time we even had a map of the Island as well as aerial photographs of our actual campsite. I was able to examine these photographs with the aid of stereoscopic equipment and obtain a three dimensional picture that enabled me to draw up a plan of the camp to scale, making use of the contours of the land exactly as they were and so avoid small depressed watercourses.

We travelled to Labuan on an American L.C.T, loading was a continuous affair, day and night, trucks, jeeps, earth moving equipment, and last of all the personnel. My mate Colin Patience was in charge of loading our gear, he was a 16 stoner with physique to match and a voice like a foghorn a real commanding personality although only a green Pilot Officer (Plt Off). Colin came back to camp to tell the C.O. he had told a Yankee Colonel off, it was a difficult job loading some items of plant. 'A Yankee bloke gave contrary orders, I told him I was in charge, and if he had anything to say to say it to me or keep out of my way.' Someone told him it was their Colonel. The C.O. told Colin to go back to the ship and finish loading. American badges of rank were a bit hard for we Aussies to follow. Sergeants, Lieutenants and Captains were easy enough, but poor old Colin, new to our own service, was completely ignorant of them.

I found it quite interesting travelling in convoy, as I am writing now in 1981 I have forgotten exactly how many ships there were in the convoy. We had HMAS *Hobart* and a couple of destroyers to look after us, it was quite spectacular to watch the destroyers racing thither and yonder through the rest of the ships, sometimes travelling in the same direction, and at other times from front to rear and when they travelled that way appearing to virtually fly through the water.

The landing on Labuan took place on Sunday, June 10th. On the evening of the 9th, the Captain of our ship had all hands; passengers and crew assembled on deck and addressed us on plans for the next day. It was quite interesting, he gave it to us, move by move so that we knew exactly what to expect and we all assembled on deck at first light next morning to watch how the assault went.

The landing took place on the Eastern side of the Island in the vicinity of the small port of Victoria, the only town that I saw at any time, although there may have been others on the island that I didn't see. There was a beach of about l–1/2 miles, and Victoria with its small harbour was at the Southern end.

At 6.00 A.M. sharp the naval barrage commenced, supported by Liberators bombing the landing area; this lasted for half an hour. During the barrage Naval torpedo boats armed with rockets prepared themselves and formed a straight line about two thousand yards off shore. Immediately the barrage stopped, the torpedo boats ran towards the shore in line abreast, about 100 yards apart, firing rockets at the rate of one every hundred yards, set to explode at 1000 yards.

The torpedo boats kept this going until they were about 100 yards from the beach, then they returned to 2,000 yards and repeated the performance. This operation we were told was known as 'Giving the beach an Admiral Nimitz haircut'. With rockets exploding at ground level 100 yards apart in both directions for a distance of 1–1/2 miles of coast line and repeating the process it was hoped there would be nothing left living above ground when the assault troops went in.

While the Naval barrage and Admiral Nimitz Haircut were in progress, infantry troops were embarking in landing craft, L.C.Ts and immediately the torpedo boats had finished their second run the L.C.Ts set out for the beach.

The only Japanese resistance that we saw from our position was one gun of sorts on an old wreck in the harbour. It fired a couple of bursts but was quickly silenced by a couple of shells from the *Hobart*. There was a solitary enemy aircraft, so high that we could hardly see it, and it dropped a couple of bombs that did no harm.

Between nine and ten o'clock the Infantry went ashore, and mid afternoon when (sic) we went in and our ship ran herself onto a dry hard sandy beach and then the blow fell. Not an enemy blow, they were too busy getting themselves hidden back in the scrub. It was an order that we were not to commence landing in case the roads became cluttered before the Infantry considered it safe to proceed to the Airstrip, which of course was the main objective.

I've been told that the language of the Skippers of the LSTs was unprintable, a couple of dozen of them shoulder to shoulder, sitting ducks in case of enemy air attack. Fortunately the enemy had nothing to attack with and intelligence must have been pretty sound on this point. It seems incredible that the ships should have been allowed to beach themselves so securely that they had no hope of getting off without either unloading or waiting for high tide.

It was not until about 9.00 P.M. that we received orders to commence landing in about four feet of water. First cab off the rank was Fred Martin, our little ginger moustached self-important 2.I.C. Fred climbed into his jeep, which had been stored aboard close to the landing platform to allow him to be first off. He started her up, ran slowly down the ramp until water reached his waist, then the jeep gave a couple of coughs and splutters and stopped dead, and Fred had to be pushed ashore.

Our vehicles had all been treated with waterproofing compound before leaving Biak by thickly applying a greasy waterproof paste over all vulnerable parts of the vehicles. As this was the first time many of our mechanics, perhaps ANY of them had ever been called upon to waterproof their vehicles there was no such thing as being able to profit from past experience. Consequently only about half of our vehicles, trucks, earthmoving equipment etc. that tried to go ashore in high tide, managed to do so under its own power.

I watched for a while and then climbed up onto the highest part of a bulldozer and got ashore with dry feet. My jeep was way back in the ship, and was brought off onto a dry beach next day. The wet landing became such a mess that it was called off until daylight to continue on a dry beach. Those vehicles that were taken ashore were parked there because it was not until about 09.00 next morning that we were advised that the Infantry had cleared the airstrip and it was safe for us to move up.

During the wet landing shemozzle it was fortunate that at least one dozer was really waterproofed and continued to work for several hours, at times with only its exhaust pipe and driver from chest up above water, pulling other vehicles onto dry land. That particular dozer, I was told finally gave up the ghost and was a complete write-off, later it was stripped and used for spare parts.

After getting ashore I made my way through mangroves to the roadside where some of our vehicles were parked, took a stretcher off a truck, set it up under the tail of the truck and slept to the best of my ability until daylight.

It was a sight to remember to see all the little lights around about where the boys were making themselves a billy of tea with the aid of 'canned heat'. This was a Jelly-like substance that we carried, each man with a small tin a bit larger than a boot polish tin. When lighted [sic] it gave off a blue flame that could be extinguished by replacing the lid and carried for further use, good for about half a dozen billies of tea before being burnt out.

When word came to move, I climbed up onto a load of motor tyres with two or three others to make the couple of miles to the airstrip. The road was very rough, and the vehicle was an earth moving type called a scraper, or carryall of about 15 or 20 cubic yard capacity. It passed under an overhanging tree; we passengers had a tremendous whack and had to hang on for dear life. I had my hat knocked off, and when I retrieved it and wiped the perspiration from my face I discovered to my horror that my spectacles were missing, they had gone right down amongst the tyres, and were retrieved, undamaged, from the bottom of the carryall when it was unloaded a week later. I could read without the aid of glasses, but had to have them to correct astigmatism and whilst I could get about my work without them, by nightfall I had the world's most distressing headache.

Going as far as I could I walked to our campsite a mile further on, a bulldozer had already gone along clearing a passage for vehicles, pushing trees out of the way and filling depressions and in my half blind state I walked straight into a swarm of wasps that had been disturbed in a tree that the dozer had uprooted, I received a couple of stings that did not contribute to my comfort or well being. It was not until the following afternoon that my jeep was brought ashore and I was able to get my gear and a pair of spectacles that American friends had given me at Milne Bay.

Our water tanker had become bogged on the outskirts of our campsite, so the cooks improvised a kitchen with some timber and tarpaulins, a marquee for a mess, and there we ate for the first couple of days until we were able to get a trafficable road into camp.

My second night ashore was spent with the cooks and a few others under a tarpaulin. I was a complete physical wreck having been without spectacles most of the day, and had no clothes other than those I was wearing as my gear was all on my jeep wherever it was. I simply made myself as comfortable as I could on a ground sheet spread on the grass between two stretchers occupied by members of the kitchen staff and spent the night there, a revolver and water bottle wrapped in a 'Hat fur felt' does not make the most comfortable pillow.

The Sergeant cook rostered his staff to keep guard, taking the midnight shifts himself. He was a particularly good type and was decorated, or rather mentioned in dispatches somewhat belatedly for service beyond the call of duty when he was on *Ambon* a couple of years earlier.

I had been able to lay out our camp on paper before leaving Biak from information gained from aerial photographs, as a consequence of which we went into action as soon as our trucks were able to reach the site.

Five ACS moving to airfield. (Photo: Tom Wilson)

Moving to airfield. (Photo: Tom Wilson)

No. 5 Airfield Construction Squadron

Don Northmore, an NCO of 5 ACS wrote:

A.C.S, and associated units of Airfield Engineers landed and camped on Morotai and soon the 2/32nd Battalion of the 9th Division and its associated units were there, while the convoys for the Tarakan-Balik-papen actions were formed and left before the end of May.

On the 3rd June, we went aboard the LSTs and other landing craft. The men boarded with weapons and gear, while the heavy equipment such as tanks, dozers, graders, trucks were below deck, all water-proofed for an amphibious landing.

After six days voyage up through the Sulu Sea, to the coast of Palawan in the Philippines, the convoy, shepherded by the destroyers, turned southward in the China Sea towards North Borneo. We watched the flying fish breaking through the waves and saw the small command vessel sailing in the middle of the convoy, for protection.

We had been briefed on the coming campaign, to expect enemy action from surface craft, submarines, and Kamikaze attacks. Ashore, we would encounter the most atrocious collection of bugs we had yet heard of and I suppose some wondered what kind of place we were being pushed into.

However, the voyage proved uneventful, excepting for episodes like that on LST 936, when some smart type turned on the fresh water (with pliers) for showers, after the Captain had ordered it off. When he discovered this, he threatened irons for the culprit and then ordered salt-water showers, and NO hot water to wash mess kit.

The result of the former was that most of the men aboard arrived at the landing with all kinds of skin eruptions, tinea, etc, which worsened as the sick bay and our medic supplies ran out, and green dye from our uniforms caused infection. The lack of hot water to wash mess kits resulted in dysentery for most, all of which could have been avoided.

On 10th June, 1945, No. 5 A.C.S. landed on 'D' day, with the 24th Brigade, A.I.F. 9th Division, when we were again under Australian Command. We had crept into Victoria Harbour before dawn and absolute quiet had to be maintained; it certainly was, under the strict U.S. naval discipline on the L.S.T.

On shore, we could see lights of vehicles travelling on a road towards a headland and as the sun rose, we found ourselves in Victoria Harbour, Labuan Island. Opposite, on our right was a white lighthouse on a green grass capped cliff, reminiscent of an English scene, but we were in the tropics.

At 7 a.m. the Australian cruiser *Hobart* opened up with broadsides from her 8" turrets, our L.S.T. along side, and the blast from the muzzles were deafening, in fact, painful to the eardrums some of the time. The bombardment lasted half an hour or so, the shell bursts ashore being seen clearly. Soon it was supported by waves of Liberator bombers and Beaufighters firing rockets, which put the ack-ack battery on the point out of action.

Two hours later, the 9th Division Infantry landed from LSTs after a few broadsides of rockets had been fired. The troops' landing was initially unopposed but resistance was soon met as they advanced towards the airstrip. Commandos had cleared the mines from the beach the day (or night) before, making the landing easier.

As we followed on up towards the airstrip, we were told the local population had been warned to evacuate the town to avoid casualties and it was rumoured that some Australian W.A.C.'s had been killed when the Japs got wind of the invasion. [Author: I can find nothing to substantiate this rumour.]

By next morning, the Japanese had been forced back to a pocket near Timbali airstrip. We had bivouacked near Labuan Airfield while the 9th Division artillery shelled the Japanese positions with their twenty-five-pounders.

We moved into our pre-selected campsites on the cliff tops adjoining the airstrip, and work commenced on getting an airfield into operation. A cursory inspection revealed that the Labuan strip had been so heavily bombed that it was impossible to repair. Therefore, it was decided that one of the main taxiways would be the basis of a new 9,000 ft. bomber strip.

Since there was no suitable coral available, it was decided to lay bitumen sealed strip. To do this, it was arranged to 'cannibalize' the remains of Victoria town and put it through a crusher to provide aggregate. There was no bitumen expert with the Wing, so they flew up an officer with this experience (from Melbourne) to do the job. He was fifty-four years of age, and soon rejoiced in the name of 'Tarpot Harry'.

The only air raids experienced in this action were one aircraft that got through to drop a bomb at the landing and in late June, an aircraft came in at dusk with navigation lights on and bombed the docks but was shot down by a night fighter.

The enemy continued to fight on in the pocket, breaking out at night

Working a 24-hr day. (Photo: Tom Wilson)

Loaded with coral. (Photo: Tom Wilson)

and mounting raids on the town and docks. They infiltrated our lines at night, creeping along the bottom of the cliffs at times, so that we had to post double sentries and set up trip wires.

One evening, a party of about forty Japs marched down the road to the docks, getting away with this bold move. They gave themselves away by arguing under a light and fighting broke out. Their object was to destroy the dock, as some had fifty-pound bombs strapped to their backs. They blew themselves up during the action in which about forty Japanese died. Before they were burnt, the war artist, Donald Friend

41

came down and made sketches. The sight preyed on his mind when he returned to his quarters with the Wing, where he shared a tent with a war correspondent.

During a storm that night, the latter got up wearing only his shorts, to shut the tent flap; the artist awoke, and thinking it was an infiltrating Jap drew his pistol and fired, hitting the correspondent in the shoulder. He was taken to 22 M.C.S. (the RAAF hospital) nearby, and nothing more was heard of the incident.

Meanwhile the Japanese were being pounded by rockets from Beaufighters and No. 5 A.C.S. was busy consolidating the new strip and pushing the extension to 9,000 feet, for heavy bombers to attack Indo China and Japan.

A few casualties occurred; LAC A W Riley of 5 A C S was killed in an accident on 26th July, a man was sniped at on the strip in a meal line. Reports of a sniper near the river resulted in the said Jap being flushed out by a patrol. The 9th Division had lost quite a few men, but not as many as expected. Photographic evidence exists that there was a mass burial of Japanese soldiers and for several years the grave of a lone unknown Japanese soldier was marked.

After the landing, aircraft came over and sprayed the countryside (and us) with D.D.T. to kill the bugs and it seemed that it was successful, for none of the worst predictions eventuated.

Work on the new Labuan Airfield continued, as the Allied attacks on the enemy home islands mounted in intensity.

The Philippines had been secured, and the Australian Task Force, under General Morshead, came under the South East Asian Command, (Mountbatten's), when it was disclosed that our next assignment was to be Indo China, which was garrisoned by many thousands of Japanese troops.

The American Air Force was bombing the Japanese mainland, especially Tokyo, with B29 bombers. The fire raids were terrible in their results, and the Japanese high command began to panic. Our knowledge of this came from the radio monitoring of Japanese and other foreign stations and we began to feel that the end, at last, was perhaps not far off.

Don Northmore concluded his recollections thus:

On the morning of the 8th August, a news bulletin obtained from the radio monitors was posted which said, 'On the 6th August, at 8 a.m., a device was exploded above the city of Hiroshima, which has been destroyed.' I remember standing there for a moment almost not digesting the significance of this. It then dawned on me what had occurred; I realized that the Allies had cracked the secret of the atom. I remember thinking that this looked like a war winner but boded no good for the future.

David Wilson wrote a book about the Airfield Construction Units of the RAAF, appropriately entitled *Always First*, which is the official motto of 5 Airfield Construction Squadron. In an extract from the book he writes of the assault landing on Labuan, describing the landing as unopposed at the time on 11th June when the Airfield Construction Squadrons landed.

It was a day of hard work and humour, against a background of 25 pound artillery firing into the hinterland. The water depth varied, averaged 60 centimetres, but there were variations, as Doug Perry of 5 A.C.S. recalls: 'When we went ashore we were directly over a bomb hole full of water. We had trouble getting the equipment out and getting it on to the beach.'

Plt Off Bennett learned this from personal experience when he stepped off the ramp of an LST – all that could be seen was a revolver held above his head as he waded ashore. To Alex Clarke of 4 A.C.S. the sight of bulldozers pressing shoreward with only exhaust pipe extensions and drivers visible above the water was memorable.

George Park remembers late in the afternoon the driver of the Survey Section Dodge Blitz buggy, Vince Sewell, negotiated the water barrier with success but was not so adept on dry land. The Blitz jammed in gear, the Army beach controller, to whom they were to report, was not impressed when Vince yelled 'I can't stop' as the vehicle hurtled past.

By 9.00 pm the LSTs had been partially unloaded; one remaining task was to roll 200 litre drums of fuel off the ramp to float ashore. The following morning when the incoming tide floated the drums some had ruptured, the reluctant men had to be threatened with disciplinary action before they stripped and entered the scum to retrieve the drums.

In the meantime a camp had been established near the airstrip. The men slept with a rifle by their side and nearby small arms fire was no joke. The airmen were each rostered to undertake one hours guard duty. Incessant artillery and small arms fire was incompatible with sleep. In the early hours the tension broke, one of the guards challenged a strange figure, when no password was forthcoming, alarmed airmen groped for rifles. The call went out 'bayonet the bastard', a terrified voice quavered from the darkness: No Not Me: I'm 4 A.C.S.' Following a call of nature the airman had little thought of remembering the word-of-the-day.

On the morning of the 12th June, the Army was pressing the enemy located around the airstrip. The two construction squadrons commenced the rejuvenation of the strip, which was a mass of bomb craters, some small, some great gaping holes nine metres deep and fifteen across. The Survey Section was up at dawn and breakfasted close to the airfield, they drank foul tasting chlorinated water as they heard the rattle of small arms fire and the rush of artillery shells overhead. Led by Fg Off John 'Dan' Daniel we walked to a position behind an earth mound at the south end of the airstrip which formed part of a revetment ... It afforded us protection as we cautiously examined the area, the fighting appeared to be taking place to the west of the strip, so we moved out. We worked feverishly all morning setting up a line of reference pegs. It wasn't easy working amongst the water filled bomb craters which was about all the airstrip consisted of at that time.

We had a brief lunch from our field rations and one of our general hands became anxious about the war being waged some little distance from us, so he climbed on top of the survey wagon for a better view. He had not been there long before he attracted gunfire, in spite of the danger we were in ourselves, we roared laughing when he fell to the ground in his haste to get down.

We took shelter in a bomb crater and shortly after several Australian infantrymen came by and expressed their surprise at our being there; it appeared the ownership of the airstrip had not been completely determined!

By the 17th June the efforts of the two construction squadrons had improved the serviceability of the airstrip to such a degree that Dakota aircraft and the first two Kittyhawks of 76 Squadron were able to land.

The reconstruction of the airfield had been difficult. 4 A.C.S. was constructing the southern portion and 5 A.C.S. the northern end; for some reason, the surveys undertaken by the two teams varied by 30 centimetres and the Wing Headquarters was called to arbitrate in favour of the 5 A.C.S. survey – a decision which did not prevent 4 A.C.S. form letting all and sundry know that the fault lay elsewhere.

DC3 stuck in mud. (Photo: Tom Wilson)

Kittyhawk. (Photo: A.W.M.)

The two squadrons used different techniques to fill bomb craters – 4 A.C.S. pumped the water out and then blasted the remaining mud out with explosives, while 5 A.C.S. simply filled the craters, but all worked a 24-hour day. The area was floodlit, warning of enemy incursions could not be heard above the noise of the machinery and plant operators were very vulnerable in the event of enemy action. Even during daylight the men were not out of harms way.

George Park noted in his diary that it was nerve-racking working steadily in light jungle to be interrupted by three or four rifle shots being fired in one's direction by an invisible assailant.

Silas Edwards kept a diary and recorded:

17/6/45 After the most chaotic week I've ever lived through we are gradually establishing something approaching order and getting a camp licked into shape. We hope to have lights into the tents by tomorrow night.

There was a thrilling sight the other afternoon when a party of A.I.F. chaps yarded some Japs into a corner in the jungle and half a dozen Beaufighters came in and 'did them over'. I was not close enough to see what was actually going on ground wise, but the 'Indian circle' of Beaufighters going round and round dishing out bursts of gun fire, one after the other, at the same target. I was to learn that Jack Durbridge was one of the Beaufighter pilots.

The works conference invariably develop [sic] into long-winded discussions about which plant should be used go on ad infinitum. Although 'Talking Shop' is against the normal rule in the Mess, but the excuse is it must be permitted as with 24 hour working it is the only time that all the officers meet.

Edwards describes the various officers: The Boy Officer, or Engineer's Apprentice; Egg-head, completely bald though still a young man, who has two topics, bulldozers and his infant son whom he hasn't yet seen as he has been up here for 14 months. Edwards recorded in his diary:

9/7/45 A comment about Japanese troops: I've seen a few prisoners in the cage; those I saw were miserable specimens of humanity. There weren't a great many Japs on Labuan. Although there may be some left in remote parts there has been no close range contact with them since the first couple of weeks.

A small party of Japs infiltrated right into the A.I.F. camp lines the other night. How they got past the perimeter guards is a bit of a mystery and what they hoped to achieve is hard to tell. There were only five of them and they were soon put out of their misery after killing a couple of Americans. Our chaps made short work of them. It was a bad show and the Americans were not impressed as the guards they got past were Australian.

1/7/45 No mail for several days, the heavy rain on the unfinished airstrip prevents the heavy aircraft from landing with the mail.

15/7/45 The painting of a timber board, a picture of a bulldozer for the mess; the Gravel Grubbers Grotto with a motto

> ABANDON RANK ALL YE WHO ENTER HERE.
> Whether Shiny-bum or shirker, or malingerer or worker,
> Whether Wing, TAAF, RAAF, or Air Board you may be
> Whether sober sir, or blotto, in the Gravel Grubber's Grotto
> You'll find nothing else but hospitality.

When Silas Edwards wrote these notes in 1981 the motto could be seen in the Australian War Memorial.

5 ACS built a church, St Stephen's. Welfare was catered for by the Army Comforts Fund; the YMCA team were from West Australia. The former staff secretary Kenneth Sykes had been taken prisoner on Crete, when with 2/7 Field Ambulance tending the sick. After a spell in a prison camp at Salonika he spent two and a half years in Thuringen PoW camp in Germany. He was repatriated with 500 prisoners and 500 medical personnel. The other two members, David Wesley and Peter Crerar, had served in the Middle East and New Guinea. Their jeep and trailer carried the slogan 'Ich Dien'. The Salvation Army chaplain was known as Honest John; he delivered a morning tea brew from his jeep and trailer.

A sports ground was laid out and named Carrs Oval; one report mentioned that thirty games of Australian Rules, soccer and rugby had been played in one week. In true Australian fashion there was usually some barracking from the boundary.

On 24th July Silas Edwards records the case of 'Lofty' Sparkes who had recently rejoined the squadron: 'He was placed on a charge yesterday for wearing shorts, which have been taboo for more than two years. Lofty had been down south and may not have known, driving a grader he had been warned a couple of times to put on long pants and roll them up above his knees, so now he will appear in Orderly Room in front of the C.O. and it will probably cost him a week's pay.'

Edwards reflected his thoughts about the end of the war and what the official policy might be regarding repatriation; authority seemed surprised that the end had come so suddenly. Without official sanction the CO decided to ease off on the work programme and take every second or third day off. Wing decided otherwise, with orders to continue as the airstrip was destined to be very busy evacuating not only Australian personnel but also the thousands of ex-prisoners of the Japanese who were expected to be liberated.

A Victory Concert was held in the airmen's recreation hut, entirely of RAAF talent, mostly amateur with a few professionals, one of whom was a tenor named Sammy Jose, described by Campbell as of outstanding quality and a glorious voice, giving quite a few popular ballads.

Gracie Fields visits. (Photo: Tom Wilson)

On 27th August Gracie Fields, accompanied by Eric Fox and vocalist Peggy Shea, gave a concert backed by members of AIF and RAAF personnel. Members of the Australian Army Medical Women's Service formed a ballet.

In his diary entry of 22nd August Edwards reveals considerable discontent in the construction squadrons: a number of officers had arranged their own postings home ahead of their turn, regardless of their time served, and it almost caused a riot. He states that in fact there was a mutiny, which would have had wide repercussions had the war not ended. It was covered up, and precipitated an official order that no personnel would go home ahead of their turn irrespective of rank. It was likely that the squadrons would be reduced to half size.

Edwards recorded on 11th September:

Yesterday a Japanese General and several high-ranking members of his staff officially surrendered to General Wooton of 9th Division A.I.F.

I went up to the strip, with quite a crowd, to watch the arrival. The Japanese aircraft circled a couple of times, dragging a long white flag of surrender. The Provost had difficulty in restraining the crowd of onlookers.

General Baba was short and stoop shouldered, not at all impressive. Both he and his officers were wearing well worn and in some instances patched uniforms.

One of his officers was quite tall, almost six foot in height, Baba was about 5'3" and his sword almost dragged on the ground. We didn't see the actual surrender of course; I was told that when the Jap handed his sword over to General Wooton the latter said, 'Thanks old chap, I've been wanting to get my hands on one of these since I reached New Guinea.'

It was Baba who ordered the notorious Sandakan death march across Borneo; he was tried as a War Criminal and hanged.

Surrender party Nakajima Ki 49 aircraft. (Photo: Tom Wilson)

Surrender party Tachikawa Ki 54 aircraft. (Photo: Tom Wilson)

Lt Gen Masao Baba, Maj Gen Kuroda. (Photo: Tom Wilson)

Submarine Action

The Royal Navy had joined American naval forces in the Pacific against the wishes of many senior American naval officers. One such unit was the 14th Submarine Flotilla. HMS *Bonaventure* had originally been laid down as a merchant vessel for the Clan Line but the Admiralty bought her for use as a submarine depot ship. She was launched in October 1942 and commissioned in January 1943.

Her first use was the main training base and depot ship for midget submarines (X craft) at Loch Striven. X craft were used in attacks on the German battleship *Tirpitz*. Following a refit the *Bonaventure* sailed to Australia via Panama Canal and Pearl Harbor during early 1945; she was part of the British Pacific Fleet, but the Americans did not approve of the use of midget submarines. At Hervey Bay, Queensland, training and trials took place to test cable-cutting operations.

In June 1945 *Bonaventure* sailed for Labuan where preparations were made for three operations:

- Operation Struggle, to place limpet mines on two Japanese cruisers in Singapore harbour, *Myoko* and *Takao*.
- Operation Foil, to cut telegraph cables in Lamma Channel, Hong Kong.
- Operation Sabre, to cut telegraph cables at Cap St Jacques, Saigon.

On 26th July three submarines left Labuan towing midget submarines. HM Submarine *Stygian* sailed from Labuan with XE3 in tow, with a passage crew aboard the midget submarine. On 30th July Lt I. Fraser RNR, Sub Lt Smith RNZVR and Ldg Seaman M. Magennis transferred from *Stygian* and slipped the tow at the eastern end of the Singapore Channel. The midget craft was navigated past shoals, wrecks and minefields for 40 miles, making five knots when on the surface. Fraser dived at 4.30 on the morning of 31st July, and three hours later he sighted the buoys which marked the boom and was able to follow a small trawler through. After nine hours submerged and nineteen without sleep Fraser began his attack on the cruiser *Takao*. The first approach failed and at 3.00 am he tried again. Magennis in frogman suit had difficulty attaching the limpet mines due to excessive marine growth on the hull. The XE3 carried two side charges each holding two tons of Amatol; the port charge dropped easily but Magennis had to return outside to release the other. The cruiser was badly damaged in the subsequent explosion and sank to the seabed. The crew made good their escape and rejoined HMS *Stygian* and were towed back to Labuan, arriving on 4th August. Fraser and Magennis were awarded the Victoria Cross and Smith the DSC.

HM Submarine *Spark* sailed for Singapore towing XE1 with the intention of sinking the cruiser *Myoko*, but this attack failed and HMS *Spark* and XE1 returned to Labuan on 5th August.

HM Submarine *Spearhead* sailed for Saigon with XE4 in tow to cut telegraph cables off Cap St Jacques. This operation was successful and sections of the two cables cut were brought back to HMS *Bonaventure* when HMS *Spearhead* and XE4 returned to Labuan on 3rd August.

HM Submarine *Selene* had sailed from the depot ship HMS *Maidstone* in Subic Bay with XE5 in tow to cut the cables off Lamma Channel. The tow failed but XE5 proceeded under its own power and succeeded in cutting the cable, although success was not confirmed until after the later fall of Hong Kong to the allies. HMS *Selene* returned to Labuan with XE5 in tow on 4th August.

On 5th August crew members of HMS *Bonaventure* were entertained ashore. On 20th August HMS *Bonaventure* left Labuan and sailed to Sydney.

HMS *Bonaventure* crew and RAAF Mosquito. (Photo: Tom Wilson)

The Australian Squadrons Arrive

In May 1945 No 77 Squadron Royal Australian Air Force, part of 81 Wing (76, 77, and 82 Squadrons) had been on Morotai Island, a part of the Moluccas group of islands. Towards the end of the month they were warned that as part of Operation Oboe the wing was to take part in the invasion of Brunei and Labuan.

The squadron embarked in Landing Craft Infantry (LCI) 753 with the pilots and rear party remaining on Morotai. The LCI arrived in Brunei Bay on 11th June and the squadron disembarked on the following afternoon. Labuan became 84 Operational Base Unit, RAAF.

The Japanese still held part of Labuan: an AIF patrol engaged a Japanese unit and the squadron's tent lines came under fire. 77 Squadron's history *Swift to Destroy* states that 'although causing considerable anxiety, no real damage was done'.

On 11th June Beaufort A9-718 of 9 Local Air Supply crashed near Sanga Sanga with the loss of Fg Off Harps-Burt, Plt Off J.F. Mooney and WO J. Simmonds. On the same day Fg Off R.P. Scott of 22 Squadron was killed.

Two RAAF Spitfire squadrons, 452 and 457, had been formed in England in 1941, and during 1942 they had returned from Europe for the defence of Australia. No 452 Squadron, based at Balikpapan, lost Flt Lt A.J. Procter in A58-465 on 2nd July following a strafing attack over Borneo, Flt Lt N.J. Cullen in A58-518 failed to return from action over Borneo on the 10th.

457 Squadron RAAF, nicknamed 'Grey Nurse Squadron', equipped with Spitfire VIIIs arrived at Labuan on 17th June 1945 and were in action two days later. Flt Lt D.E. Evans escaped uninjured when Spitfire A58-629 crash-landed on 7th July; another was damaged beyond repair one week later. On the 18th three Spitfires of 457 Squadron were written off; the undercarriage of A58-614 collapsed on landing following a combat sortie. During heavy rain at 11.20 A58-616 crash-landed; immediately afterwards A58-618 tried to land on the reduced strip, slid into mud, the airscrew dug in and the aircraft broke in half.

On 19th June Beaufighter A8-114 of 31 Squadron made the squadron's last recorded strike against Kuching radio station. On 20th June two Spitfires of 457 Squadron, Flt Lt G. Campbell (A58-620) and Flt Lt Scrimgeour

Bogged Spitfire. (Photo: Tom Wilson)

(A58-631), shared the kill of the last Japanese Mitsubishi Ki-46 Dinah shot down near Sipiitang. AC 1 Clarke of 457 was killed at Labuan in an accident on 23rd June. LAC F.I. McInerny of Air Supply was killed in an accident on 1st July.

The first 82 Squadron Kittyhawk landed on 25th June, the remainder arriving on 3rd July.

> The first of 77 Squadron's Kittyhawks arrived at Labuan on 30 June and the Squadron set about making the site more habitable. A vegetable garden was set up and for ten days all members worked on reconstruction of the road between the strip and the camp area.
>
> The first operation, an attack on Keningau and Sapong (North Borneo) took place on 3rd July. The Squadron suffered its first casualty since arrival at Labuan. Flt Lt H. Cooper in (A29-827) was killed on 15th July following a strafing run against an enemy held position at Ranau. The rest of July was spent attacking Japanese targets in North Borneo and flying armed reconnaissance. [*Swift to Destroy* page 15]

77 Squadron were not alone; 76 Squadron had lost Plt Off L. Collins on 26th June in (A29-1154) and W O W.P. George on 19th July. 82 Squadron lost Fg Off W.H. Day on 26th July.

F.W. (Fred) Barnes, who as an Air Vice Marshal became Deputy Chief of the Air Staff RAAF before retiring, recalls a practice flight in Kittyhawk A29-1055 on 20th July and bombing and strafing Melalap in the same aircraft on the 26th. On 2nd August in A29-1002 he strafed Sibu and on 13th August Bintulu in the same aircraft.

On 11th July the engine of Spitfire A58-633 of 457 Squadron failed over Borneo; the pilot Fg Off F.J. Inger bailed out near the coast, sheltered in the jungle and was rescued on the following day by a Catalina.

Kittyhawk losses continued: A29-704 crashed on landing when returning from an Army Cooperation flight on 13th July. On the 17th A29-614 was damaged on landing and was not repaired.

On 14th July Spitfire A58-606 suffered damage from anti-aircraft fire over Kenningau and belly-landed at Labuan. Three days later Spitfire A58-629 was written off following a landing accident.

Catalina A24-365 of the 42 Squadron detachment based at Labuan carried out the squadron's last operation of the war during the night of 26–27th July: a mine laying mission in the Banka Strait

No 1 Squadron RAAF had formed in January 1945 and arrived with their new Mosquito aircraft during June and July, ready for their first 'bash' as current slang had it. On 19th July the squadron suffered the first of many taxiing and landing accidents caused by Labuan's mud. A52-526, the aircraft involved, had been the first Mosquito to fire guns in anger against the Japanese in New Guinea. The squadron flew 65 sorties from Labuan between 8th and 15th of August. No 1 Squadron lost a Mosquito A52-510 on 9th August when it crashed in enemy held territory.

RAAF Mosquito. (Photo: A.W.M.)

Mosquito No1 Squadron RAAF. (Photo: Tom Wilson)

No 4 Squadron RAAF were equipped with the CAC Boomerang, an aircraft originally designed for home defence. The Chief designer, Fred David, a Jewish refugee from Austria, had worked pre-war for Heinkel in Germany and Mitsubishi and Aicha in Japan. The project to use as many components as possible from the Wirraway resulted in a small heavily armed fighter with two 20-mm cannon and four .303 machine-guns mounted in the wings. With the arrival of American and British fighters it was relegated, quite successfully, to a close support role.

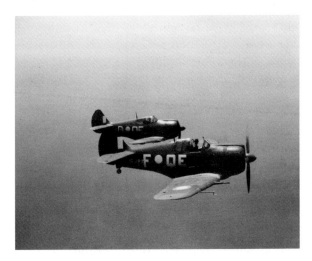

CAC Boomerang. (Photo: A.W.M.)

The squadron arrived at Labuan on 23rd June. One aircraft at Labuan, A46-121, had previously been modified for low-level oblique photography with two cameras mounted in modified belly tanks. On 29th July A46-195 crashed at Labuan. LAC Guerin died in an accident at Labuan on 31st July. On 2nd August two Boomerangs of 4 Squadron had landing accidents in the mud; they were not repaired.

93 Squadron ground party arrived at Labuan aboard SS *Simon Bamberger* on 13th July from Morotai. The first aircraft arrived later and on their first operation, 26th July, two Beaufighters of 93 Squadron, A8-87 and A8-123 took off from Labuan to accompany a Mosquito on an armed reconnaissance, targets of opportunity were strafed and the Sibu residency was rocketed. The rest of 93 Squadron arrived with nineteen Beaufighters on 5th August to become part of 86 Wing.

Two days later an 800-ton Japanese tanker was reported near Kuching. Eight Beaufighter crews of 93 Squadron attacked it before going on to strafe Trombol airfield. Sqn Ldr Gulliver led the attack in A8-122 followed by Flt Lt Sims and Fg Off Farrant in A8-85; the latter aircraft flew into debris and crashed in enemy-occupied jungle. The tanker was last seen listing badly and claimed as destroyed; later the tanker was stated to be in fact the private yacht of the Rajah of Sarawak. Sims and Farrant were rescued by a Catalina on 21st August. The squadron had flown its last operation on 13th August.

On 3rd August 77 Squadron personnel had been told of peace overtures by the Japanese; they were kept informed over the five-day rest period.

13 Squadron RAAF arrived in August with Ventura and 'Beaufreighter' aircraft (see below). Modified for light transport duties, they were engaged in supply and evacuation of prisoners of war. The squadron adopted two abandoned aircraft, a Mitsubishi Ki 51 'Sonia' and a Nakajima Ki 27 'Nate'. The squadron eventually disbanded at Labuan on 11th January 1946.

No 82 Squadron's most successful strike during this period occurred in mid-August when several Kittyhawks caught Japanese aircraft about to take off from Kuching airfield. Four enemy aircraft were destroyed and two others damaged before the fighters turned their attention to barge traffic on the Sarawak River.

76 Squadron carried out their last operation on 14th August, strafing Japanese aircraft at Keningau.

On the 16th August 93 Squadron lost a Beaufighter when A8-129 stalled short of the runway; the pilot WO J H Ellers and navigator W O A C Dunn were injured but survived. Two days later Mosquito A52-520 crashed on take-off and was not repaired. [Source ADF Serials]

'The end was heard over the public address system on 16th August when

Surrendered Mitsubishi Ki-51. (Photo: A.W.M.)

the broadcast by Mr Clement Attlee was relayed. On the following night a victory party was held in the Airmen's Mess, with the cost being borne by the Officers Mess.'

War ends. (Photo: Tom Wilson)

On 16th August Warrant Officer Lionel Parham flew low in a Beaufighter from Labuan over the Kuching compound, dropped leaflets and reported about sixty prisoners of war. Later a Mosquito crew saw a message 'A.I.F. All Well Here' laid out in white letters. A Beaufort crew, escorted by Mosquito, confirmed this following a low-level detailed reconnaissance. Medical supplies, clothing and food dropped from a DC 3 were seen by escorting Mosquito aircraft to have fallen into the compound. At Kuching the first aircraft to land after capitulation of the Japanese garrison force was a Kittyhawk from Labuan to pick up photographs and return them to Labuan for onward transmission to Australia.

Preparations were now in hand to re-take Singapore. Nine RAAF Catalina (11 and 20 Squadrons) left Labuan with 1000 pounds of blood plasma, penicillin, quinine and other medical supplies to care for thousands of prisoners of war. Of the 5000 held in Singapore 1200 were known to be in urgent need of medical treatment. RAAF Dakotas were used to transport an army wireless unit of thirty men and their equipment to report on the progress of the liberation of prisoners

On 18th August Mosquito A52-520 of 1 Squadron collided with a Kitty hawk A29-608. Mud remained a problem, 1 Squadron lost another Mosquito A52-500 on 24th August when the aircraft slewed sideways during a take-off run; it was stripped for components. On 28th August Kittyhawk A29-702 of 82 Squadron crashed at Labuan with fuel problems; this aircraft was also reduced to components.

During August 77 Squadron was commanded by Flt Lt A.B. Taylor, in A Flight; on 25th and 29th August Fred Barnes flew practice formations in Kittyhawks A29-1032 and A29-804. In the latter aircraft he flew further practice formations on 3rd and 5th of September. By that time 77 was under the command of Flt Lt R.P. Curtis.

The very crowded airstrip had further aircraft losses. On the 29th August Beaufighter A8-121 taxied into a Mosquito. During take-off a tyre burst on Mosquito A52-511, the aircraft made a successful belly-landing later with no injury to Fg Off Orr or Plt Off Ryan.

Although the formal surrender of Japan as a nation was signed aboard USS *Missouri* on 3rd September, the surrender of all Japanese forces had not been finalised. Leaflets were dropped to the enemy forces calling on them to lay down their arms, informing them of the Emperor's capitulation, and instructing them how to behave and where to report for the signing of surrender terms.

On 12th September Fred Barnes of 77 Squadron was one of the pilots flying cover of the army occupation of the Kuching PoW camp. He flew further practice formation flights and on 20th September recorded his last operational flight from Labuan in Kittyhawk A29-1012 in a reconnaissance over Melalap, Sapong Keningau and Ranau.

An Australian radio station, 9AF, was set up on Labuan in August 1945. Later in October, probably by use of captured Japanese equipment, Station JL2 operated from the back of a three-ton truck.

Thanksgiving service. (Photo: Tom Wilson)

Flown to Labuan in Auster aircraft of No 16 Air Observation Post RAAF from Ranau were three surviving Australian prisoners of war; Private Nelson Short; W O William H Sticpewich and Private Keith Botterill, escapees who survived out of 2700 in total, 1900 of whom were Australian, who took part in the death march from Sandakan to Ranau.

Three Sandakan survivors arrive at Labuan. (Photo: Tom Wilson)

In preparation for the end of the Japanese occupation an organisation called Recovery of Allied Prisoners of War & Internees (RAPWI) had been set up. The former prisoners from Kuching were taken to Labuan as shipping became available, to be given medical care at the Australian Field Hospital while waiting transport home. The sick were evacuated first followed by families with children. Many former prisoners anxiously awaiting return to their homes nicknamed RAPWI 'Retain All Prisoners of War Indefinitely'.

Agnes Keith described the overloaded C47 as taking three hours from Kuching. At Labuan they found their ex-guards confined; she reported that the sergeant-major met with a fatal accident. Lieutenant Nekata attempted suicide, cut his throat, was nursed back to life to await his trial, eventually to be executed by hanging. Keith tells of Celia and Bill Taylor: 'In spite of ill health Celia was described as one of the bravest, least selfish, and most hard working, steadfastly believing that she would find her husband alive at the end of the war.'

Dr Taylor had been sent from Kuching and imprisoned in Singapore; ill and weak from abuse he survived long enough to be freed. He had tried, but could get no news of his wife so he decided to return to Australia and wait for news there. He was flown to Labuan to await a plane, where he came upon his wife also awaiting passage to Australia. A fleet of Dakotas operated from Morotai and Labuan to return prisoners from Singapore to mainland Australia.

The Keith family spent five days in Labuan in a camp at the far end of the island from Port Victoria; the camp was approached by DUKW at low tide only. They were then flown out to the Philippines aboard a US Navy PBY.

The Official Surrender of Japanese 37th Army by Lieutenant General Baba Masao took place at Labuan on 10th September 1945 before Major General G.F. Wootten Commander of 9th Australian Division. The Surrender delegation had arrived in a Tachikawa KI-54C (Hickory) aircraft.

Colonel Suga, the Commandant of Kuching and Sandakan prisoner of war camps, was brought to Labuan by flying boat on 13th September 1945 to face war crimes investigation. He committed suicide on 17th September. Colonel Aikyn, commander of the Japanese Miri garrison, hanged himself at the Labuan PoW compound.

Japanese war crimes trials took place in 1946. Labuan was one of eight venues of Australian led war crime trials; details are in the papers of Captain Hon. Atholl Randolph Moffitt CMG of the British Borneo Civil Affairs Unit attached to HQ 9th A.I.F. Labuan. The British tried nineteen cases for war crimes, twenty-nine people were accused, thirteen sentenced to death, ten of these sentences were confirmed, one was given a life sentence, twelve were imprisoned for various terms and three were found not guilty [WO 235/813-1117].

Reg Solway, of Swindon, who served post war at RAF Changi, recalled serving aboard a troopship *Highland Brigade* and calling at Labuan in October 1945 with fresh troops from Sydney; former prisoners of war and internees were then taken to Singapore for repatriation.

Royal Australian Air Force Base 84 OBU

84 Operational Base Unit now faced several tasks, continuing the evacuation of prisoners of war, returning men and materials to Australia and converting Kittyhawk squadrons to the recently introduced Mustang.

On 29th August 1945 it had been announced that 81 Wing Units, including 77 Squadron were going to Japan as part of the British Commonwealth Occupation Force. Volunteers were called for, but out of the 200 personnel in 77 Squadron only thirty-six volunteered.

September started with another crash on the 2nd when Auster A11-19 of 16 AOP crashed and was reduced to components. On return from a training flight on 8th September Kittyhawk A29-1002 of 77 Squadron swung into soft ground and was stripped for components. A flight of Beaufighters over Kuching as a show of strength took place on 11th September; A8-123 was missing from the twelve planned as it had become bogged in mud before take-off.

No 81 Wing received its first Mustangs on 12th September, from the then disbanding, 84 Squadron. Pilot conversion courses began on the following day for the pilots who had elected to go to Japan. The conversion from Kittyhawk to Mustang was expected to take two months, but was to prove a much greater task than originally thought. The tendency to swing due to torque effect was greater with the Merlin engine than the Allison engine of the Kittyhawk. During the initial conversion period there were several accidents. Fred Barnes commenced his Mustang conversion in A68-551 on 22nd September with stalls, and on the following three days aerobatics, pairs formation, battle climbs and high-level bombing.

On 22nd September A9-708 Beaufort of 9 Communication Unit crashed on landing. Beauforts manufactured in Australia were fitted with Pratt and Whitney Twin Wasp engines; forty-six of these were later converted to Mk 9 configuration by fairing over the fuselage and fitting seats, and were renumbered in the A9-700 series and unofficially named Beaufreighters.

The first Mustang loss was on 29th September when A68-762 of 82 Squadron failed to return after an oxygen climb exercise. Fred Barnes flew a Kittyhawk A29-1012 during the search for the missing pilot, F/Sgt A.J. (Junior) Hunter.

Mustang fighter. (Photo: A.W.M.)

Beaufreighter. (Photo: A.W.M.)

Beaufreighter. (Photo: Tom Wilson)

77 Squadron's first accident occurred on 7th October 1945 when Fg Off K. Crawford (A68-711) crashed due to a strong cross wind. The pilot escaped unharmed but the aircraft was written off.

Mosquito A52-509 of 1 Squadron crashed during take-off on a non-operational flight on 1st October; the aircraft was reduced to components. Later in the month Mosquito A52-512 had engine and undercarriage problems and was ditched in the sea off Labuan.

During October 77 was commanded by Flt Lt I.E. Crossing; all Kittyhawk flying by then was being carried out by pilots who had nominated discharge or return to Australia. 77 Squadron's last mission was flown on 6th October when two aircraft made a tactical reconnaissance of Sapong and Keningau where Japanese troops were sighted heading south between Keneingau and Tambumen, all carrying heavy packs.

Fg Off Maddern of 4 Squadron successfully crash-landed Kittyhawk A29-451 on a beach on 16th October, thirty miles south of Jesselton.

77 Squadron suffered two further landing accidents after which both Mustangs needed substantial repairs. A68-705 landed with engine problems on the 19th and after heavy braking nosed over; the aircraft later served in Japan and Korea.

By the end of October all 77 Squadron pilots had converted to the Mustang. Fred Barnes flew ten flights during the month on air test and several formation flights. The majority of the ground crew had attended courses at No 22 Repair and Salvage Unit. On 30th October 77 Squadron had a strength of twenty-one Mustangs and had flown 220 hours for that month. The last incident recorded for the month was on the 29th, when Beaufighter A8-230 crashed due to a flat tyre.

A59-76, a Lockheed Ventura of 13 Squadron which had been nominated for use in Japan, swung on take-off on 10th November and was damaged beyond repair. On 11th November Kittyhawks left for No 6 Aircraft Depot at Oakley, Queensland, where they were scrapped. Beaufighters A8-201, 256 and 283 were allocated to escort single engine aircraft back to Australia. Kittyhawks known to have returned were A29-906 and 908; A29-1051 had left Labuan for Australia but was reported missing fifty miles from Morotai on 21st September 1945.

Mustang A68-747 of 76 Squadron ran off the airstrip on 14th November and hit a coral mound; it was repaired and later used in Japan. Beaufighter A8-247 returning with a starboard engine problem crash-landed on the 15th.

A Beaufighter A8-173 of 93 Squadron swung during take-off on 20th November and crashed. Another swing during take-off resulted in Mustang A68-727 of 77 Squadron being written off on 28th November. Fg Off R.B. Birrell of 76 Squadron had left Palawau for Labuan on the 28th in Mustang A68-771 and was reported missing.

The Beaufighter was used occasionally as a fast communications transport. On 10th December a 93 Squadron Beaufighter A8-184 swung on take-off, hit loose earth at the side of the runway, bounced over two Mustangs and collided with two Mustangs, A68-761 and A68-714, shearing off their engines. The pilot of the Beaufighter was thrown clear but the aircraft burst into flames and the passengers were killed. Six RAAF personnel died as a result of this accident, including the OC 86 Wing, Group Captain Holswich, and the CO of 93 Squadron, Squadron Leader D. Gulliver, Flight Lieutenant J.M. Harris, Fg Off D.J. Seekamp, and LACs Herrick and Nash.

Mr Frank Lees gave a first-hand account of this very tragic accident that happened when the squadron was based in Labuan before going to Japan in 1945:

I owe my life to Honest John, the Salvation Army chaplain who each morning from his jeep and trailer gave us our morning brew on the strip at Labuan, North Borneo, in 1945.

As an aircraft electrician I had been in the landing at Balikpapan,

Borneo, and responsible for wiring up the airstrip lights and camp lighting for 38 0BU. When the Japanese surrendered I accepted the opportunity to serve with 77 Squadron Mustangs in the British Commonwealth Occupation Force in Japan.

My first flight was in a Mitchell bomber from Balikpapan to Labuan. My duties on Mustangs at Labuan included servicing the battery located in front of the cockpit bulkhead. To service the battery the electrician stood near the wing's leading edge and that's where I was on a typical tropical (but not humid) morning around 10.30 am one morning.

My mate AC Dickson was in a similar position standing on the next aircraft, my aircraft was A68-714. Eighty-one Wing, 76, 77, and 82 squadrons shared the strip with a Beaufighter squadron which had pranged about five aircraft in a month.

Standing on our Mustangs we would observe take-offs in front of our parked line of Mustangs, with interest. On this memorable morning, an aircraft was revving up at the end of the strip when I saw Honest John's jeep approaching the area in front of the tower. I immediately called across to my mate Clive Dickson to get off his aircraft and have a brew. He refused, so I badgered him with strong words. He relented and together we climbed down.

At the back of our aircraft we observed a Beaufighter roaring down the strip. As it approached it veered to starboard and clipped the engines and propellers of our Mustangs. It sheared the engine off A68-714 and threw the battery on the ground where it had fallen intact. The Beaufighter careered down the strip and caught fire, the pilot was thrown clear but died the next day.

We manhandled the fire truck through the mud to the aircraft and heard and witnessed the tragedy of fellow airmen dying, as the Beaufighter burned, our fire truck was so bogged that we were helpless. My electrician mate who lives in Melbourne, claims that I saved his life. In reply I tell him that we both owe our lives to the Salvos and in turn I suspect the Salvos would say God gave us a few more years.

Sqn Ldr R.P. Curtis assumed command of 77 Squadron in December. Fred Barnes flew several sorties in various Mustang on formation flights, gunnery practice, cross country flights and wing tank tests during the three months before leaving for Japan. These flights were in seven different aircraft, including nine in what became his personal aircraft for the flight to Japan A68-788. Mustang A68-735 failed to take off on 14th December and was not repaired.

Crashed Beaufighter. (Photo: Tom Wilson)

In January 1946 the base disposed of several Kittyhawks by burning the unserviceable remnants of the following ten Kittyhawk A29s: 607, 614, 625, 652, 656, 676, 828, 903, 905, and 907. It is interesting to see how the destruction of these aircraft was carefully documented; it occurs to me that there might well have been what was known in later years as creative accounting, in view of how many Kittyhawks lay mouldering in nearby tidal waters for several years.

Scrapped aircraft. (Photo: Brian Roche)

In addition to pilot conversion, rifle drill was carried out and a Japanese language course was conducted by a Japanese army major, Major Dayasakai, a prisoner of war. In mid-January packing started for the move to Japan; on the 21st all personnel attended familiarisation lectures on the Japanese people and their customs. The SS *Murrumbidgee* docked on 8th February to load squadron vehicles. Two days later the squadron's personnel boarded HMS *Glangyle*, setting sail the following day. Five ACS sailed for Japan on 11th February.

Meanwhile the pilots and rear party prepared for the long ferry flight; the camp hygiene was carried out by Japanese PoWs. Due to lack of accommodation at Clark Field in the Philippines the departure date was constantly delayed. On 4th and 5th March the pilots got as far as strapping themselves into their aircraft, only to be delayed again due to bad weather. The other squadrons, 76 and 82 were also delayed.

Finally on 11th March 1946 the first formation of fifteen 77 Squadron Mustangs set off, followed an hour later by another fifteen, the ground crews following by C 47 aircraft. One Mustang A743 of 82 Squadron was written off on 13th March due to battery acid damage.

Fred Barnes left Labuan for Clark Field in A68-788 on 11th March, was delayed at Clark Field and left on 17th March for Naha, Okinawa, arriving in Bofu, Japan on 21st March.

In extremely bad weather on 18th March 1946 one group of 81 Wing aircraft, a Mosquito A52-147 escorting Mustangs of 82 Squadron A68-718, 770 and 773, were lost. It is believed that they flew into the sea; some wreckage and the bodies of the Mustang pilots were recovered. Two days later a Mustang A68-751 of 76 Squadron en route from Labuan to Japan was written off when a truck at Clark Field in the Philippines drove across the path of the aircraft during take-off. A Mosquito A52-609 was destroyed when it swung during take-off on 4th April; it was about to escort aircraft of 87 Squadron from Labuan to Australia.

The British Return

Just prior to the Japanese capitulation in August 1945 Lord Louis Mountbatten GCVO CB DSO Supreme Commander of South East Asia Command (SEAC) was told that the boundaries of his command would be extended to include Borneo, Java, the Celebes and part of Indo China, formerly in SWPA. In January 1946 as the Australians withdrew this was formalised, but it was decided to continue martial law. Mountbatten visited Labuan on 8th December 1945.

The original plan for the British occupation of Borneo entailed one brigade group of 20 Indian Division moving to Borneo; the relief of Australian forces was originally planned to start in October. Events in the Netherlands East Indies, where the Japanese had promised independence to the Indonesians, meant a fierce campaign against what was initially regarded as an insurgency, involving British troops and RAF units.

The task eventually fell to 32 Indian Infantry Brigade, planned to arrive in November, reaching Labuan at the end of December 1945. During 1945 the brigade had fought the Japanese army in Burma, had moved to Indo China to protect French interests and had been harried by the Viet-Minh. Brigade headquarters would be at Labuan with a battalion each at Jesselton, Brunei and Kuching, scale of clothing to be 'east of Brahmaputra'.

From Saigon the 9/14th Battalion Punjab Regiment sailed for Kuching, and the 4/2 Ghurkha to Jesselton aboard SS *Arunda*, each with their attached units. The remainder of the brigade, 3/8 Ghurkha, 114 Field Regiment, 92 Field Company and 59 Field Ambulance sailed aboard MV *Highland Brigade*, arriving at Labuan on 30th December. The commander and staff had arrived in HMS *Nith*; this vessel, originally an anti-submarine escort, had been converted for the Normandy landings as a brigade headquarters ship.

The brigade HQ was established in the Government House area of Labuan, with the role of ensuring the internal security of the country, exercising military administration, and controlling, guarding and eventually arranging the evacuation of the Japanese who had been disarmed. Control of Japanese present was through HQ 37 Army; included in the total of 30,000 in Borneo and Sarawak were 500 navy personnel and 5000 civilians [WO

172/7098]. The brigade would take over from 20 Brigade AIF, part of the Australian 9 Division. Many Australian infantrymen sailed for Australia aboard HMS *Vengeance*, a Royal Navy aircraft carrier in January 1946.

Conditions were described in the Brigade War Diary, this from a unit that had recently served in Burma and Indo-China, as very poor with much bomb damage, probably in a state of devastation unequalled throughout the British Empire; an estimated 6000 displaced people who were poorly clad, undernourished, and suffering from malnutrition and tropical diseases.

The British Civil Affairs Unit (BMA) arrived at Labuan from the ship *Ingleburn* in January 1946, a party of sixteen officers and forty-two soldiers. The unit produced and published a Military Administration Gazette; the first was by command of Brigadier W.J.V. Windeyer commanding 9 Australian Division and dealt with postage; the second dealt with prices and rent control. Succeeding Gazettes covered courts and registration of societies; followed by more on police and magistrate appointments and rubber dealers. The seaplane tender was operated and refuelled by BMA, the coxswain being provided by Shell Oil Company [WO 172/ 10044].

In February 1946 a Policy Directive was issued on repatriation of Japanese civilians; Japanese settlement in British Borneo was of long standing. There were a number of Japanese settlers before 1914, and between 1919 and 1939 this number increased. The number of Japanese in Sarawak was 150 in 1940 and according to the 1931 census 450 in North Borneo, but at the time of the Japanese invasion there were 2000 Japanese and 1000 Formosans in North Borneo. Some 700 Japanese, men and women, were employed by the Borneo Fishing Co – a Japanese concern. The remainder were employed by the large Japanese rubber and hemp estates on the east coast, or were small holders growing rubber and hemp. Outwardly the Japanese were good settlers, industrious and law-abiding.

The directive considered the possibility of permitting Japanese permanently resident since 1930, Japanese women and their children married to citizens of British Borneo, female former citizens, who had married Japanese and Formosans who had been permanently resident since 1938 to remain in the country, should they wish to, provided that there was no evidence that they were undesirable. A screening mission from SEAC would list the persons above against whom nothing was known; any person who appeared to have a genuine claim to be allowed to remain, and those considered undesirable [WO 32/11166].

In March 1946 rifles were handed in and Japanese booty sold by auction. On 27th May 1946 the 32 Indian Infantry Brigade embarked for India, certain units remaining.

The British Military Administration gradually returned matters to a civil footing. The State of Brunei was handed over to a civilian government on 6th July 1946.

On 15th July 1946 Acting Governor Mr James Calder assumed the government of the new Colony of North Borneo and British Military Administration ceased. The first Colonial Office appointed Governor of British North Borneo, E.F. Twining CMG MBE, arrived in February 1947.

The Royal Air Force on Labuan Post War

The RAF were present, initially, to establish an air link to enable recovery of the colony to a peace-time basis. This detachment over the years functioned as a staging post for RAF flights, a small base for photographic survey, a listening post and eventually a fully fledged RAF operational base during the Confrontation with Indonesia.

The first post-war RAF contingent would comprise SHQ Labuan with 340 personnel, 110 Squadron, 7110 Servicing Echelon and an embarkation unit and a detachment of 230 Squadron Sunderland flying boats, for which sheltered alighting runs for two or three miles were reported in all directions. A suitable Group Captain was to be selected by 300 Group as Officer Commanding RAF Borneo.

300 (Transport) Group RAF had been formed in Australia to support the British Pacific Fleet; 243 Squadron operated fifteen Dakotas, supported by 4243 Servicing Echelon; 1315 Flight operated Liberators; they were joined briefly by No 238 Squadron, also equipped with Dakota aircraft.

As the allies of SWPA advanced a number of staging posts were set up. The route from Sydney to Singapore was opened in November 1945, via Balikpapan and Labuan, and small servicing parties were flown in. Labuan with one officer and one airman became 191 Staging Post. Dakota KN 547 flew down the route from 18th December carrying Christmas cheer.

Don Henderson, who had earlier ferried Maryland, Baltimore, Ventura and Marauder aircraft from Nassau via Belim and Natal to Accra, was a Dakota pilot on 243 Squadron based at Camden. He flew the route Cloncurry, Darwin, Timor, Balikpapan, Labuan to Hong Kong via Saigon in January 1946.

Advanced Group Headquarters were set up in Hong Kong. During January 1946 No 238 Squadron disbanded. Flt Lt G.A. Day carried out a staff visit to Labuan, as did Flt Lt J. Hall, a Signals Branch specialist. It was decided that the High Speed Auto Link, Melbourne to Labuan should be retained. 300 Group was disbanded in the early months of 1946 [AIR 25/1064].

There were many changes as the assembled forces moved from the original war footing to occupation and towards a peace-time establishment.

These plans were all affected by reduction and disbandment of units and changes in the Headquarter's structures, and further by repatriation of personnel.

Ken Dix, an armourer on 110 Squadron, sent me a copy of an article in *The Union Jack*, a forces newspaper, probably written in late 1945 or early 1946 by Sqn Ldr B. Mycock:

PEACE FLIES IN TO LABUAN

Labuan – tropical island just north of the Equator. On the one hand an idyllic seascape that might never have known the inferno of modern war: on the other Jap prisoners and the wreckage of a broken dream of Asiatic domination.

The RAF is here now, and its job is to take over the working of the coral airstrip as yet another link in the vast chain of service airways in the Far East. The Australians are pulling out – many to their homeland and some too for the occupation of Japan. They give us the legacy of a fine coral strip, two thousand yards long, which will be a link in the airways between Malaya, China, Australia and the Philippines. Labuan will remain a tiny island spot on the map of the Far East but it will be an active and vital spot. It may become a calling place for some of the civil airlines of land planes or flying boats, or it may – the decision is yet to be made – become a permanent RAF base.

Law and Order

The immediate job of the RAF party is to set up a headquarters, to take over the running of the Staging Post and to house a fighter squadron which will help to maintain law and order on Borneo – the third largest island in the world. It is a pretty full programme but the officers and men are tackling it with enthusiasm. They have as their CO Group-Capt F.C. Sturgiss OBE, who has 22 years experience in the RAF as a pilot of flying boats, a specialist in aerial photography and an administrative organiser.

The Australians have been here for some eight months and have contrived with very unpromising material to make themselves pretty comfortable. It was evidently hard going at first. Although the landing in May 1945 was virtually unopposed [sic] it had been preceded by an intense bombardment with shells and rockets which 'rubbed out' the village of Labuan [sic] and wrecked almost all the buildings around the airstrip.

But though Labuan has been a blood drenched island it is peaceful enough now. The staging post is operating for the Dakotas, Sunderlands and Catalinas that fly through this base. Three Sunderland flying boats are using the moorings near the airfield. It is proposed that they will eventually take over a daily 'grocery run' which is now done by the Australian Catalinas.

Pre-War Threads

They supply isolated garrisons, parties of British officials who are back to work in British North Borneo picking up the pre-war threads and remote communities which must depend on air supply for the time being. The whole problem of flying over Borneo is one of considerable difficulty. Navigators tell of many peaks rising over 17,000 feet, which are not on the charts. It is densely tropical country for the most part and though in the coastal belts the natives of the northern part are strongly pro-British there are in the hinterland tribes of pigmy cannibals whose temper and behaviour are, to say the least, uncertain.

Meanwhile the airmen tramp up and down the sandy path to the cove, passing with no more than a glance at a small wooden cross half hidden in long grass by the side of the track. It bears the inscription 'Unknown Jap Soldier killed 16.6.45'. That was war; this is peace and reconstruction.

A later cutting was sent by Ken Dix:

Perils in Paradise
Routine Orders at Labuan North Borneo – the RAF's newest station in the Far East – are a guide to the snags of life on romantic tropical isles.

The Station Commander Group Capt F.C. Sturgiss has warned the men in a station order that 'they are not to sit under coconut trees'. Coconuts are very heavy and have a long way to fall.

'They are not to swim out far from shore.' There are sharks in the deeper water just looking for a meal.

'They are not to go out into the jungle or long undergrowth in shorts or without a shirt; and they must not bathe in the nude.'

The first RAF unit on Labuan had a shortlived stay. In October 1945 104 Embarkation Unit RAF (Flt Lt S.H. Kingaby) sailed from Madras for Sumatra aboard HT *Samothrace* in early November but were diverted and offloaded at Port Swettenham. Ordered to embark with SHQ *Brunei* for Borneo, the unit entrained on 25th December 1945 and embarked for Labuan. 291 personnel aboard MT *Circassia* landed on 12th January. 1946 personnel ex 36 PTC *Calcutta* aboard HMS *Sefton* landed on 16th January 1946.

SHQ Labuan, originally titled SHQ Brunei, took over the domestic accommodation from Australian Tactical Air Force and then moved with 230 Squadron Detachment to a site vacated by the US navy. The unit was visited by the AOCinC Air Chief Marshal Sir Keith Park KCB OBE MC DFC RAF.

The 230 Squadron Sunderland detachment had first arrived in January 1946 aboard RN *304/S*, followed a few days later by Sqn Ldr K.W. Nicholson in 230/X as O C Detachment. Two other pilots known to be a part of this detachment were Fl/Lts Elliot and Briggs. One Sunderland ML797 Q is pictured at Labuan in Tom Docherty's book about 230 Squadron, *Hunt Like A Tiger*. This aircraft was one of the last RAF flying boats to fly at RAF Seletar in June 1959 and was selected to be flown home to UK for preservation, but the lack of route facilities meant that it joined the other Sunderlands and was scrapped.

Duties included local reconnaissance, re-establishing District Officers to their posts, and on occasion transporting Japanese war criminals from Kuching to Pontiniak for trial. On 21st January Flt Lt Elliot of 230 Squadron made a first attempt to deliver supplies to a starving group in the mainland mountains, but cloud cover was too extensive. Leaving at first light a successful drop of 741 packages weighing 7000 lb was made on the following day.

To service the flying boats a detachment left Seletar, embarking on SS *Empire Marshall*, consisting of a coxswain, one motor boat crew (MBC), two marine fitters, one electrician. These tradesmen accompanied a refueller, a seaplane tender and a dumb dinghy for duty at Labuan.

RAF Station Seletar ORB notes daily Sunderland flights of 209 or 230 Squadron from Seletar to Labuan with passengers and freight, or to Hong Kong via Labuan. These flights were not without loss: Sunderland U/209 crashed near Sembawang shortly after take-off with the loss of five crew and eight passengers.

In February 1946, 104 Embarkation Unit unloaded 1000 packages for 7110 Servicing Echelon. The establishment of fifty-three civilian labourers was largely filled by Japanese prisoners of war.

An unusual visitor in February was Sunderland L/240 Squadron from its normal base in Ceylon (now Sri Lanka) en route to Makassar, Sulawesi; the squadron was disbanded during the following month.

In March came the order that the embarkation unit would disband on 30th April and that all RAF personnel and stores were to be moved. The first men left in LSTs 403 and 408 and HMS *Glenroy* during the month. During April more men and nearly 900 tons of stores left for Singapore in five separate shipments, leaving an establishment of one officer and eleven airmen. In May 1946 Flying Officer Challoner assumed command and in June 1946 the 104 Embarkation Unit was disbanded [AIR29/19].

A weekly Sunderland air service was instigated by the BMA commencing 27th May 1946, leaving Singapore on Thursdays for Kuching and Labuan, spending the night at Labuan and returning to Singapore via Kuching on Fridays. This aircraft would be available for diversion to Sandakan if so authorised.

An Air Priorities Board was set up in the event of dispute, but invariably those dictated by ACSEA had to be adhered to. The OC RAF Detachment had a seat on this board. Flt Lt J.L. Lindsay was appointed Air Transport Officer for BMA; guided by OC RAF Detachment he was directly responsible for all freight and passengers carried on the Sunderland aircraft. There was no charge for civilians or serving personnel, but all passengers had to sign an indemnity.

110 Squadron RAF had an even briefer first visit to Labuan, equipped with Mosquito VI aircraft and supported by 7110 Servicing Echelon a detachment arrived in December 1945. 110 had the honour to have been the first RAF squadron to engage in offensive operations against Germany on 4th September 1939, attacking German shipping off Wilhelmshaven, and to have made the final RAF offensive operation of the war on 20th August 1945. Flt Lt Peter Maddox, a navigator (W), had been with 110 since August of 1944. He first flew into Labuan on 12th December 1945 and they stayed for two nights.

There had been evidence of structural problems with the Mosquito aircraft in humid conditions for some time and on 11th January 1946 all Mosquitos were grounded until modified by RAF Seletar.

Ken Dix had served since 1941 as an armourer and had been with 110 for three years. He had very bad skin problems and had been advised to apply for a medical return to the UK, but he felt the squadron was such a family that he did not want to leave. He disembarked from MT *Circassia* on 12th January 1946. It was not long since the Australians had left and 110 occupied their tents, which Ken Dix remembers as being quite comfortable. There were occasional cricket games against the Indian army unit.

110 Squadron Mosquito line. (Photo: Ken Dix)

The squadron ORB noted that 'ground crew airmen had arrived in small parties and were loaned to SHQ to supervise Jap prisoners of war in moving ammunition. There was disruption at Seletar caused by a strike; the strike committee chose not to interrupt the movement of the squadron's ground party'. Higher authority had asked that the disruption caused by airmen frustrated by slow demobilisation should not be called a strike.

Victoria. (Photo: Ken Dix)

Victoria harbour. (Photo: Ken Dix)

Recalling his posting, Ken had no memory of any strike at Seletar. Prisoners of war were brought daily by the Indian army soldiers to work as cleaners. One prisoner, Panaka by name, a university-educated man from Hiroshima, had a fair grasp of English and was appointed in charge of the cleaners. Ken said that when the squadron left on disbandment the prisoner was in tears.

On 15th January W O East was killed when he fell from a truck returning from a swimming trip; W O de Boer was injured.

On 30th January Flt Lt Foss air tested a Mosquito together with F/Sgt E.S. Willis RAAF. The aircraft was seen to pass overhead with the port engine feathered. Ken was among the airmen who later found wreckage of the burnt-out aircraft in the south-east of the island; both airmen were buried at Labuan on the following day.

Peter Maddox had flown back to Labuan on 31st January and was engaged in the search for Flt Lt Foss' aircraft. The remainder of the squadron followed in four separate groups during February; the working day was established as 06.00 to 13.00. On the 4th February Flt Lt Levy and Fg Off Shorts arrived with Mosquito TE 606 from Allahabad, a total flying time of 10 hours 40 minutes.

On 27th February Flt Lt Collins and Fg Off Read searched for Japanese prisoners who had escaped from the island by boat, but they could find no trace. Early in March they searched again; this time they were armed and ordered to fire if the boat was seen. Ken recalled arming the Mosquito going to search for escaping prisoners of war, but there was no sign of the boat and the search was called off.

Flt Lt Harding and Fg Off Read air tested a RAAF Beaufighter A19-705, and later also air tested Beaufighter A19-726. These two aircraft left for Melbourne early in March.

One Mosquito crash-landed in the jungle; the crew had supplies parachuted to them by Flt Lt Abel in Sunderland 230/Z. It has been difficult to identify the aircraft. Ken does remember the incident, but has no firm details – was it perhaps an Australian aircraft?

Following notification that the squadron was to disband, equipment was loaded at the docks for return to Singapore. 110 Squadron disbanded on 15th April 1946. Ken left Labuan aboard SS *Rajuah* for Singapore on 3rd May 1946 and shortly afterwards to Calcutta for posting back to the UK.

Reginald Allen, a LAC electrician, served on Labuan during 1946–47; he had served on Bomber Command during 1943–44 until he was drafted to Einewetok. Eight Liberty ships with twenty-one airmen aboard each ship sailed via Panama with the aim of setting up a British bomber base. Came the atom bomb and Reginald was sent to Hong Kong to help in disarming the Japanese, where he marched on the Victory parade. From Seletar, by Sunderland aircraft, he was posted to Labuan where he maintained generators for the signals detachment.

At Labuan he befriended Fr de Witt, a Dutch priest who had started the local orphanage, with nine orphans. Fr Francis Sint, born in the Tyrol, had taken home leave in 1939. He returned to Borneo in 1946 and assisted in the Labuan orphanage.

Travelling home via Suez, Reginald's war took him around the world. Fr de Witt returned to Europe in 1947 after he contracted TB and visited Reginald at his home in the UK. Fr de Witt did return to Borneo in 1951, but sad to say he was murdered by robbers in Kudat, Sabah in August 1983.

The late Ken Appleford, who in later years became a Shackleton captain and retired as a squadron leader recalled visiting Labuan during his tour on 209 Squadron, based at RAF Seletar, from April 1946 until Sept 48, flying Sunderland Mk Vs. 'Throughout that period many sorties were flown around North Borneo, carrying freight and passengers (including civilian) to and from places like Kuching, Labuan, Jesselton and Sandakan. Labuan was our refuelling point. If we stayed the night at Labuan I would remain on board as boat guard, later our night stops would be at Jesselton. The airstrip at Labuan was not cleared for civilian aircraft until much later, hence our commitment to passengers and freight East of Singapore.'

Jack Dent, a Fitter II (E) had joined 209 Squadron at Koggala in Ceylon as they converted from the Catalina to the Sunderland V early in 1945. The squadron set off for Hong Kong. Jack's aircraft damaged a float when alighting at Penang, and they met fierce weather at Hainan and were held there for a week by Chinese troops. At Hong Kong part of the squadron formed 88 Squadron. Jack stayed with 209 and moved to Seletar, Singapore.

Writing in *Searchlight*, the RAF Seletar Association newsletter, in 2008, Jack recalled being flown to Labuan on 5th July, for a 'few' days, with Sgt Short and George Flack to rectify an engine problem with the CO's Sunderland M. After a six-hour flight they moored next to the u/s aircraft, and next morning the CO flew back to Seletar, leaving behind a pilot and flight engineer. The oil filter was found to be blocked, as was the engine and a signal sent to order a new engine, accessories, plus a few home comforts. Jack recalls 'a docking area for unloading cargo and oil from small freighters, a huge stretch of beach, a large rough air-strip, a detachment of RAF communications personnel (12 in all) working in wooden huts but living quite comfortably in large well equipped tents, plus about a hundred Indian Army Engineers and their officers.

'The aircraft was in a small lagoon away from the sea, but still the tides affected the depth of the water under the boat from deep to a few feet. We decided to sleep aboard, after all, there were berths available, plenty of room to move about, and that infamous paraffin stove in the galley.'

The following morning they rose early, opened up the leading edges around the starboard inner engine, erecting the portable jib to begin removal of the duff motor. How to get the perishing thing to shore 600 yards away. After some consultation they borrowed a DUKW (a six-wheeled amphibious vehicle) from the Indian Army; Jack took a day's course on the vehicle and they also borrowed a Jeep.

By the third day, with the DUKW positioned under the starboard wing and ready to receive the engine, George lowered the gantry chains; Tom Short and Jack eased the load down. As the engine touched down so the lightened starboard wing rose, until there was no more slack left in the chain, the port float being pushed deeper into the water. Panic stations ensued, with thoughts of three airmen facing court martial for sinking a Sunderland, but they soon had the engine back in its bearers.

Next day was spent scrounging sandbags from their Indian Army friends to counterbalance the weight as the engine was removed. As the night tide came in they could hear splashing as sand fell from the wing; they were losing ballast as the boat rocked. It was decided to sleep ashore for the rest of their stay.

They were made welcome, the tents had decent beds, good lighting and a fair size 'fridge'. The cookhouse was efficient and the meals excellent.

On 18th July the CO Wg Cdr Ogle-Skan was flying K on a courier and staff visit. He took off from Jesselton on three engines and M was cannibalised for an oil pipe at Labuan before he could return to Singapore. (AIR 27/2461)

A replacement engine arrived by Dakota, was loaded on the DUKW, the trickiest job being to safely manoeuvre the vehicle between the fuselage and float. The new engine was fired up on 8th September by the pilot and flight engineer, who then took off. Shortly after the flight engineer called 'loss of oil pressure starboard outer, feathering prop'; the other engine had seized, and there followed a long taxi back to the mooring. They signalled for another engine and started with another removal. Jack wrote that he was enjoying their 'little trip' by now.

While waiting they were ordered to marshal four Dakotas; nobody was sure why they were coming. All four were lined up and about 100 fully armed soldiers disembarked. Three officers enquired the whereabouts of the rioting Indian Army. The RAF officers appeared; there had been mis-interpretation of a signal saying the island was being taken over! Jack writes that the aircraft finally departed with a lot of red faces all round.

In due course the engine was delivered, fitted and successfully air tested, and Seletar notified. The CO collected the aircraft, and Jack and his colleagues returned after a two-month 'holiday'. The CO presented Jack and his three colleagues with a silver lapel badge as a reward for their hard work.

(J) Gerry Payne was a F/Sgt flight engineer on 209 Squadron at this time and recalls flying on Wg Cdr Ogle-Skan's aircraft in June 1946 to take a general to Borneo. Gerry cooked a meal for the general in the galley during the five-and-half-hour flight. He thinks it might have been a stew; he had to refuse the great man a second helping. Gerry regularly flew the Borneo courier service with passengers and freight; on one occasion they flew the Governor's wife, and some time later took the pregnant lady back to hospital in Singapore.

Evacuation from Labuan had originally been considered in December 1945, with an arrangement with the local authority that the airstrip would be maintained. Handover to the civil administration was considerably delayed as the military administration was still in control of Borneo and Labuan. It was necessary, therefore, to retain an air service while military administration continued, and it was considered likely to continue until May 1946.

Once 110 Squadron were withdrawn Labuan would be retained as a staging post until the last army unit left. Owing to shortage of personnel and MT on the staging post a request was made for personnel to be attached ex 110 squadron. The RAAF and RNZAF were to fly in support of their units in Japan via Morotai, Philippines and Okinawa; Labuan would therefore serve no useful purpose.

Air Commodore Whitley asked for both a short- and long-term policy decision to be made. He suggested in view of the strategic position that Labuan be retained on a semi-permanent basis for use during periodic deployment of Strategic Reserves [AIR23/2386].

Photographic Survey

In April 1947 a nine-man detachment from 81 Squadron, RAF Seletar was sent to Labuan to service a rotation of Mosquito PR34 to be engaged in a photographic survey of British North Borneo, operating on a three-day cycle.

Like all units at that time there was imbalance in manning and serviceable aircraft; 81 were short of navigators. My brother Nav 2, Bale, recently trained on Beaufighter maritime duties, had arrived in Singapore to serve on 84 Squadron, and was told to report to 81 who needed navigators. Jeff Jefford in his excellent history of 45 Squadron *The Flying Camels* relates that 45, then based in Ceylon, loaned three navigators to help on the survey. One of them, Fg Off Drake, noted, 'our PR OTU was ten minutes on the back of a fag packet in the crew room', which was probably all that my brother had.

The first sortie would be flown from Seletar, landing at Labuan from where the second flight would be made with a return to Labuan. The final sortie would be flown from Labuan, landing back at Seletar. Aircraft serials RG 230, RG 255 and RG 284 are recorded as taking part in this operation.

Initially all areas briefed were cloud-covered. The survey continued through May and June. Of the thirty-eight sorties in July 1947, fifteen were aborted.

The Squadron CO Sqn Ldr Merrifield and his navigator W O Radford were engaged in a survey of Sarawak when the aircraft lost glycol so they diverted to Labuan.

During June six villagers were bitten by a mad dog, but there was no serum available at Labuan. An 84 Squadron Beaufighter airborne from Singapore was diverted to pick up the only available serum at Kuala Lumpur; this was flown to Singapore for onward delivery to Labuan by a 81 Squadron Mosquito. It was later reported that the serum was successful and that the villagers had recovered.

Paul Trotter, an AC1 photographer at that time, recalls serving on various 81 Squadron detachments: ' … undoubtedly Labuan was the jewel in the crown, a most amazing experience, at that time just an airstrip (ex Japanese liberated by the Australians), much equipment left all over the place, jeeps, DUKWs etc and some Japanese aircraft heavily stripped for souvenirs.

The DUKWs proved to be most useful to and from the Sunderland service.'

Paul continues, 'There was no flying control, negligible fire or ambulance facility, although there was an ex Aussie fire truck it was almost inoperable and no hope in an emergency.'

For a large part of the time Paul was the only photographer, but recalls having a corporal to supervise him at some time. He fitted, tested and loaded K17 (US) cameras and removed exposed film in total darkness in a dismounted Brownhall Photographic trailer and putting the film into tins to be taken back to Singapore by the next Sunderland.

Paul recalls 'the arrival of a USAF Fortress photo ship and supporting DC-3, the first thing offloaded was a proper refrigerator, we had a kerosene operated one which only kept the beer tepid. The CO of the USAF detachment took personal mail back for England to USA via Manila which proved to be quicker than Forces Mail.'

Accommodation was Spartan. 'Aircrew lived in a house (of sorts) the airmen lived in tents, with a trench around the outside. There were a few staff, some cookhouse fellows, with local assistance and a couple of "Sparks" who manned the radio shack. The cookhouse and leisure area had a good roof and sides of fine wire mesh to keep the insects out. Various 16mm films arrived by Sunderland, one being a Glenn Miller, the photographer being expected to act as a projectionist, the Glenn Miller sound track was popular and re run several times.

'Ablutions were an ongoing problem, old oil drums were set in the ground under a corrugated roof shelter with a plank to sit on. Every now and then someone used to put aviation fuel into the drums and set fire to it, having first removed the plank.

'During a visit to the bay by three ships of the Royal Navy, the 81 detachment were invited aboard and some rum was consumed. During the Naval visit 81 made a habit of very low passes on returning to the island.'

On 23rd August 1947 two 81 Squadron Mosquitoes were unable to land as the airfield was closed by an intense storm. Both aircraft crash-landed, RG306 landing one mile south of Papar, RG307 twenty miles north of Jesselton; the crews were unhurt. The F540 quotes both aircraft as serial No RG307, stating that one film magazine was saved, the other destroyed.

Paul Trotter recalls this incident and remembers 'that another Mosquito climbed above the storm and returned to Labuan, the PR blue paint was stripped off almost down to the wood, like sandpaper, the pilot, Monty Walton, and navigator were OK, but quite pale faced.' One other Mosquito known to have been at Labuan during August was RG283.

The detachment resumed in September, considering the survey to be seventy-five per cent complete, detachment members returning to Singapore on 21st September, by which time 81 Squadron had moved to Changi.

Despite more surveys by 81 and a 58 Squadron detachment from the UK, over the years mapping had still not been completed by the time of Confrontation and it was necessary for surveyors of the Royal Engineers to provide locally accurate maps.

Leaving Tengah on 13th January 1948, Operation Snapdragon, the ferry and escort of six Spitfires for 28 Squadron, accompanied by Mosquito RG 308 Fg Off Price and Nav 2 Bale as navigation cover were ferried through Labuan to test the feasibility of reinforcing Hong Kong. They flew to Clark Field on the following day, recalled to Clark Field on the 15th, reaching Kai Tak on the 16th.

In that same month 81 Squadron moved again, this time to Tengah. Mosquito RG 308 returned to Labuan on 31st January following a survey of New Territories and delay after a single engine landing at Nichols Field and subsequent repair.

On 16th February of that year Mosquito PR34 of 81 Squadron detachment returned in order to complete the aerial survey. On 9th March spares and mail arrived for the squadron in Beaufighter RD 803. Fg Off Price and Nav 2 Bale joined the survey for the remainder of the month, variously flying RG 308 and VL 614 for just under 500 exposures in March. The April survey was considered to be a great success; the Price/Bale crew flew on twelve days taking over 1300 exposures, leaving Labuan on 15th May after another nine days of survey flying.

During that detachment a letter was sent to the *Daily Mirror*: Dear Sir while walking in the jungle recently a black disc was found. It was about a foot in diameter and appeared to have many grooves, it was later found that it was one continuous groove that ran from the edge to the centre. IS THIS A RECORD??

Fg Off Price/ Nav 2 Bale in VL 614 were one of five Mosquitoes that staged through in late May and June en route to Hong Kong, from where they were to assist the French in a survey of French Indo China. This detachment was cut short by the aircraft being recalled to Singapore when the State of Emergency was declared.

RAF Changi transport aircraft carried out a weekly supply flight to Labuan during the early part of 1948; the weekly flight ceased on 26th May and reverted to a monthly routine.

The Far East Flying Boat Wing post war comprised Nos 88, 205 and 209 Squadrons; the latter two were based at RAF Seletar. 88 Squadron had been reformed as a Sunderland squadron in the transport role and was based at Kai Tak as a transport link with occupation forces in Japan.

On 1st February 1948 Flt Lt Letford DSO, DFC flew B/88 to Labuan from Jesselton and left on the 4th for Hong Kong. In May he flew the same route in the same aircraft. 88 Squadron Sunderlands captained by W O Rhodes flew the Seletar-Jesselton-Labuan-Hong Kong route on 17th and 25th May and again on 1st and 7th June. The last record in F 540 of 88 Squadron on this route during 1948 is a flight by Pilot2 Bartrum on 23rd November.

On 1st June 1948 Flt Lt K.V.F. Lucy of Air Command Far East visited RAF Base Seletar in connection with parenting responsibility for Labuan.

Basil (Jack) Frost was a wireless operator straight from his training course at Compton Bassett, who had left UK for Ceylon aboard RMS *Dunera* in March 1948. Just before reaching Colombo his posting was changed to Changi. In late July he was detached to Labuan, leaving Seletar in a Sunderland flying boat on the 'Borneo Courier'. Departure at that time was on Monday morning, calling at Kuching and Labuan with a night stop at Jesselton. On Tuesday the Sunderland flew to Sandakan, returning to Jesselton for another night stop. The return journey to Seletar was via Labuan and Kuching. On Jack's flight he was invited to spend some time on the flight deck; the first stop was at Kuching. Jack arrived at Labuan mid-afternoon to be taken ashore by the harbour master's launch and then by truck to the camp. The camp was on the edge of jungle and consisted of wooden sheds serving as the wireless cabin, medical store and general store rooms. There was also a building used as the cookhouse, mess room, recreation room and mini cinema, which Jack recalls often broke down.

Complement consisted of one officer (Flt Lt Scott), a corporal medic who Jack claims was in charge of the box of plasters, a wireless mechanic and four wireless operators who worked shifts. There were a few other airmen and a cook who was assisted by local employees. Jack also clearly remembers the villager who had the job of emptying the latrine buckets; he used to walk along head held high (I wonder why) as if he owned the place, with a yoke across his shoulders and bucket at each end. Jack was puzzled by his black bowler hat worn as if he was something in the City. The transport comprised a few bicycles and an old truck that was maintained by an Indian civilian; Jack claims that he worked wonders on it. The OC had a dog called Hoover, because he would pick up anything that reached the floor. The pet monkey was called Chinta (sweetheart).

Jack shared a tent with two other wireless ops, Alan Daniels and Vic Chambers. They often tried to hit the small lizards running along the tent top frame, seldom succeeding. One of the 'old hands' told him he had missed something special – the week before they had had an iguana. When Jack asked what had happened he was told they had chopped its head off.

The signals link was controlled from Changi and consisted of Labuan (ZT9), Jesselton, Hong Kong (Kai Tak) and Manila, but traffic was not very busy. The set most regularly used was an AR 88 on 8885 Kcs. The Mosquitos of 81 Squadron were also worked while airborne; Jack found the NavW's morse to be very slow at eight words per minute, compared to a normal rate of twenty words. They would reply in plain speech giving their ETA over the strip and sure enough they would roar over the W/T cabin at treetop height with that lovely Rolls Royce Merlin sound.

Jack describes the main street of Victoria as consisting of rows of open-fronted shops, made of wood, rather like very large boxes laid on their sides. There were jewellers, a tailor, food shops and a barber's shop where the two attractive Chinese girls often interrupted the haircut to wind up the old gramophone. Another early impression was of seeing an old Chinese lady walking with great difficulty – she had bound feet, Jack could not understand how such pain could be inflicted deliberately. Her feet were no more than a few inches long.

He recalls a serious accident in the harbour when a seaman had fallen into the hold and needed hospital treatment. The injured man was flown to Singapore in a DC 3 aircraft that was at Labuan; the aircraft left during a torrential downpour. Watching the take-off Jack saw it disappear from sight with the tail wheel still firmly on the ground. He never heard how the victim got on but thought the RAF did him proud.

Catalina, 1947. (Photo: Basil Frost)

C-46 Commando, 1948. (Photo: Basil Frost)

RAF detachment, 1948. (Photo: Basil Frost)

Jack was interested in the various aircraft that staged through Labuan. RAF and USAF Dakotas were the principal visitors, and he noted one civilian Dakota of Kearsley Airways (G-AKDT) from Stansted. This aircraft had been doing cargo work around the Far East and was on the way to take part in the Berlin Airlift; the airmen at Labuan told the crew they would have loved to have hitched a lift back home. The first American aircraft that Jack worked were a US Coastguard Catalina, a US C-46 Commando and a Beechcraft Expeditor. Jack was surprised at the size of the Curtiss C-46 Commando.

Victoria, 1948. (Photo: Basil Frost)

Like many servicemen based on Labuan, Jack visited the Australian War Cemetery and was impressed by their sacrifice; at that time several landing craft remained on the beach slowly rusting away. Some of Jack's friends decided to walk through nearby jungle and shortly after found an almost intact Beaufort 'just lying in the foliage, it had been converted into a light transport and communication configuration by having its mid upper gun turret removed and the fuselage had been fared down to the fin. The a/c was virtually complete and undamaged.'

The plane had either overshot on landing or perhaps it had lost power on take-off or stalled when trying to do a go around [sic]. Either way it was in good condition, we rather foolishly climbed all over and inside it and had a great time doing it. The a/c had just belly flopped on the dense foliage which had acted as a cushion, in fact I'm sure the wheels were not touching the ground and the jungle was starting to grow over it. What a find that would be today – the engines and propellers were undamaged would be worth a fortune alone but that was sixty years ago and it is doubtful if any of it survives today.

It is likely that this aircraft was Mk9 (Beaufreighter) A9-708 of 9 Communication Unit, which crashed on landing, without loss of life, on 22nd September 1945.

Changi Detachment

The first acknowledgment in Changi records of a detachment at Labuan is in January 1949, with mention of a collection of books and gramophone records being forwarded. Sqn Ldr Green carried out an airfield inspection. A fitting party from Radio Repair Squadron Seletar installed an H/F Direction Finding station on the old Jap strip and H/F W/T and VHF equipment during January.

On 7th February 1949 Flt Lt H.E. Gundry was posted for duty at Labuan. A De Haviland Vampire was being demonstrated in the Far East and flew via Labuan en route to a demonstration in the Philippines; the aircraft was delayed awaiting brake spares at Labuan on the return leg. There was one further flight by 230 Squadron recorded as carrying seven passengers to Labuan in March 1949. During May ten Spitfires of 28 Squadron flew to their new base in Hong Kong, stopping at Labuan overnight.

Laurie Bean on the RAF Forum website states: 'I know from the 209 Squadron ORB that up until May 1949, 209 Squadron was tasked with the "Borneo Courier" flights.'

The last was flown by the Squadron CO, Sqn Ldr P.R. Hatfield in Sunderland VB882/W, and left Seletar on 23rd May calling at Kuching and Labuan before arriving at Jessleton. On the 25th they flew on from Jessleton to Sandakan and Tawau before returning the same day to Jessleton. The return trip to Seletar was flown on the 26th via Labuan and Kuching.

The June 1949 ORB entry shows the following 'Borneo Courier' flight stats: 143 round trips; 245 flying hours; 368,000 nautical miles travelled; 7000 passengers; 286,000 lb of freight carried.

With the airfield now being open to civil aircraft, Malayan Airways took over this task. In June the Education Officer from Changi visited to arrange correspondence courses for the RAF Education Test, followed in July by two equipment officers.

In 1949 consideration was given to the defence of Borneo, the necessity of dual-purpose guns at Jesselton and Labuan, and seaward defences, noting the coral airstrip at Labuan and the need for fighter aircraft with attendant ops/control room.

Civil Aviation

Civil aviation was gradually developing in the region. Kuching airport was officially opened in September 1950 with a runway of 1372 metres in length. In September 1951 Air Headquarters wrote to the Director of Civil Aviation expressing concern that the Labuan runway was breaking up and in urgent need of attention.

During July 1952 the Ministry of Civil Aviation (MCA) wrote to the Colonial Office noting that the International Civil Aviation Organisation (ICAO) regional plan had identified serious deficiencies with the airfield and called for immediate improvements to the surface, found to be rough and deteriorating by the six flights per week by DC-3 and DC-4 aircraft. The five operators at that time were Malayan Airways, QEA, who used Labuan for their Sydney-Tokyo route, Cathay, Garuda and Air France.

MCA declined a request to contribute $150,000, the matter being left to the Colonial Office. In August the colonial authorities were asked if the work had been completed, the Governor's Deputy replying that completion was not likely to be made until early 1953. Captain Grey of QEA strongly recommended sealing the ends and the provision of turning loops. Further he stated that in view of the high temperatures and local atmospheric conditions the runway should be lengthened.

In November of that year MCA reported that Labuan had again been discussed in the Air Navigation Commission of ICAO in Melbourne. The Australian government considered the runway to be too narrow. Further, MCA were concerned they would be unable to argue that 90 feet was wide enough should the matter be raised again, neither would MCA be able to contribute to the cost.

On 8th December the Governor reported to the Commissioner General that the sealing of three hundred yards of touchdown points would be carried out and improvement of the surface was under consideration.

The Governor reported to the Secretary of State for the Colonies on 9th April 1953 that work to seal the touchdown areas had duly been completed, but he admitted that the remaining 4200 feet was placing a strain on the resources of Public Works Department (PWD). He feared that with continuing surface attrition the strip was deteriorating and was likely to call for further urgent work to ensure aircraft safety.

Mr A.W. Savage, the Director of Civil Aviation, Malaya/Borneo, advised that the point was approaching where the airfield must either be enlarged and maintained to ICAO B1 standards, or use of the airfield must be restricted, in the near future to aircraft of less than 35,000 lb all-up weight. The Governor further reminded the Secretary of State that Labuan had recently been declared an international airport, at that time the only such airport in British Borneo. Its location on the long-distance great circle routes and its excellent weather conditions and approaches made Labuan an extremely attractive staging post on long distance routes, not only for the RAF, but for a number of 'foreign' operators of which Qantas, Air France and Garuda were at that time the most important.

In less than five years traffic had increased from one Malayan Airways Dakota a week to 298 movements a month in March 1953. The number of aircraft movements had increased in the previous three years from 1527 in 1950, to 3594 in 1952. The principal movements in March had been RAF Valettas, Qantas DC-4s, Garuda Convairs, Air France DC-4s and Shell Company Prince. The Governor regretted that KLM and Air France had not been permitted to land Constellation airliners on trans world routes.

The Governor proposed that, in view of the importance of the Labuan airfield, plans for early implementation should be made to develop the airport to satisfactory standards, in order not only that existing traffic be maintained, but also that potentially available traffic should be attracted. He had been advised that if the requisite improvements were made the first probable increase would be Constellation and DC4 aircraft taking immigrant traffic from Europe to Australia; furthermore it was highly likely that 'soft' currency operators staging through Manila at that time might be attracted to Labuan to avoid paying landing fees in hard currency. Failing further development there was reason to fear that an alternative airfield might be developed elsewhere.

Although no recent bearing tests had been carried out, the 1949 test indicated that the runway was probably strong enough to receive aircraft up to 110,000 lb all-up weight. While the length was sufficient for Constellation and probably for Comets, the current width precluded such traffic. The Governor sought funding as the probable cost could not be justified from the colony's resources and asked for pressure to be brought to bear on the Ministry of Transport. He added that the RAF maintained a detachment at Labuan and that plans were well advanced for considerable development of the RAF Station in conjunction with the RAAF. Service use was considerable: in the period June 1952 to March 1953 there had been 971 civil and 504 service movements. He suggested that Labuan should be regarded as joint-user airfield and that the Air Ministry should contribute. He also asked for Air Ministry assistance in preparing the necessary estimates.

The Commissioner-General had informed him that the Commanders-in-Chief regarded the development of Labuan airfield as a necessary step in connection with the defence of the region.

The Air Ministry stated that they had no requirements for the development of Labuan, but only for the maintenance at its existing standard. The RAF used it purely for staging purposes, with one Valetta a day and occasional irregular flights; the width and other characteristics were adequate for their purposes. The figures of military movements quoted included all military movements; the present military use of Labuan was mainly due to the Korean War and would be substantially reduced when it ended. In the absence of any operational squadrons based at Labuan, the Air Ministry would not be prepared to consider a joint user contribution, and they would be most reluctant to put in staff to run the ground services at the airfield. They expected to use existing facilities in the colonies free of charge for staging aircraft in the interests of Commonwealth defence where no extra expenditure was involved to meet purely RAF requirements. If the Governor decided to allow the airfield to fall below its existing standard, or to close it down completely, they might have to reconsider their position. If the Governor decided to go ahead with development of the airfield, the Air Ministry would be willing to carry out an initial survey at cost, but would not prepare a detailed plan unless Air Ministry Works Directorate were to carry out the required work.

At a meeting in May 1953 to discuss the future of Labuan airfield it was learned that KLM would have liked to use the airfield for a great circle route from Bangkok to Darwin, and that Qantas wished to stage through en route to Hong Kong. The MCA insisted on runway widening to 150 feet.

In 1955 the Department of Civil Aviation and Meteorological Services, responsible for British Borneo Territories, was formed to cover Sarawak, Brunei and Labuan with headquarters at Jesselton (Kota Kinabulu).

In more recent times Labuan airport has been expanded, with the potential to handle over a million passengers per year, but currently handles less than half those numbers. A plan to become a regional hub for connecting flights has been postponed.

The Fifties

At the end of the war the Brooke family had ceded power to the British and Sarawak became a crown colony. Following considerable unrest the Governor, Mr Duncan Stewart, was assassinated. The late Peter Weston, then a Signaller 2 on 45 Squadron recalled:

It was decided that a show of force was needed, so a force of 5 Brigands of 45 Squadron and 4 Tempests of 33 Squadron from Tengah, and 4 Mosquitos from the P. R. Unit (81 Squadron) based at Seletar, were despatched on the 12th of January 1950. I was in the leading Brigand with Flt Lt. Dalton Golding, with the Brigands leading, followed by the Mosquitos and then the Tempests. We flew to Kuching, the Capital of Sarawak, (more like a small village in England), where we turned north following the coast, flying at about 1000 feet in loose formation, until we came to a settlement or one of the many oilfields, when we would drop down to 200 feet over places such as Sibu, Miri, and others not marked on our maps. We passed the huge oilfields of Brunei for a few minutes then turned back to Brunei where we were to turn West across the sea to the very small island of Labuan.

The airfield had just the one runway of crushed coral, rolled fairly hard, and was in the region of 2000yds. The amenities were quite primitive but bearable. The Australian airlines, mainly 'Quantus' [sic], were responsible for its being, they used it for a re-fuelling stop on their cross-pacific flights. We departed the next morning to overhead Brunei, then turn toward Kuching. As we were approaching the oil fields at Sibu the leader gave the order to close in, i.e., a tighter formation, which was done. While we were passing at low level it was fascinating to see the huge flames coming from the very high burn off stacks, but unfortunately, one of the Mosquito pilots also may have been intrigued, because as I was looking out to the rear, the aircraft on the port side of the leading Mosquito very gently eased up and sliced the complete tail off, they both immediately dived into the ground, it remains so vivid in my mind. I informed the pilot and then the R/T came alive, our leader asked one of the Mosquitos to stay and circle the crash site and report later, we had to continue on because having 11 aircraft circle the site would be useless.

We could not reach anyone at Kuching; we were out of V.H.F. range at that point although I kept trying. Finally we made contact and later when we were approaching Kuching; they called us to inform that the occupants of the 2 Mosquitos did not survive. Sadly, we made our way back to Tengah.

The squadron ORB reported:

On 13th January 1950 two Mosquitoes of 81 Squadron, PF624 and RG254 practising for a display collided over Jesselton, four aircrew, Flt Lt Carpenter, Fg Off Barber, Nav 2 Wallace and Nav 3 Pointer were all killed. They are buried in Kuala Belait cemetery, Brunei.

A second flag-waving trip was ordered later in February, which only involved 45 Squadron; five Brigand aircraft made a night stop at Labuan on 23rd February.

In February 1 Flight of 81 Squadron was detached to Labuan comprising four officers, four aircrew, twenty-one airmen and four soldiers; the detachment was expected to last from March until 1st September. At the same time a conference was held at Air Headquarters (AHQ) to discuss Labuan's requirements.

General Sir John and Lady Harding visited Labuan, Jesselton and Kuching in May. During the following month the weekly Tuesday courier/supply flight started again, and further members of 81 Squadron arrived. Fg Off G Meyrick took up duty as OC Detachment in July 1950. In August he recorded in F 540 the visits of Sqn Ldrs J.J. Walsh and Stewart of Far East Air Force (FEAF) to the Detachment on the Government Monthly Courier. Air Marshal Jones, Chief of Air Staff RAAF was entertained by the unit on Saturday the 19th, while the Qantas Empire Airways (QEA) aircraft was refuelling. A visit was made to the Australian War Grave Cemetery and an inspection made of the runway.

Two visits were made by Sunderlands of 205 Squadron on the 15th and 23rd. An inspection was made of the unit on the 29th by Group Captain Fuller-Good, Officer Commanding, RAF Changi.

In late August Air Vice Marshal Mellersh KBE, AFC attended a defence meeting at Jesselton. Considering the defence of Labuan airfield, the Governor raised the lack of telephone connection between Labuan and Jesselton and the need for establishment of an air route from Singapore to Hong

Kong via Labuan. In the matter of Aeradio the RAF would still be responsible for aircraft approaching from Darwin and the H/F beacon.

On the following day AVM Mellersh flew from Jesselton on a Far East Communication Squadron aircraft; the District Officer, P.W.B. Officer and Chief of Police were in attendance. An inspection was made of the Aircraft Control and hotel buildings [AIR 23/8562].

In September a supply drop was carried out by the monthly courier at Pensiangan, an inland rural town some 20 kilometres from the Indonesian border. Photographs of the operation were distributed to government departments. The liberation of Labuan was celebrated on 9th September. His Excellency the Governor and Lady Hone attended the six events, three of which were organised by the RAF Detachment.

A flight of six Dakota aircraft of 38 Squadron RAAF carrying Royal Marines refuelled en route to Japan and Korea. On return these aircraft carried 81 Squadron personnel and stores back to Singapore, following the completion of that survey, the intention being to revert to one Courier flight per month.

A premature opening of the Control Building was necessary after a storm wrecked the old building. The Signals Detachment worked fifty-one military and forty-nine civilian aircraft during the month.

In October a successful supply drop was made to the northeast of Beaufort by the Monthly Courier. Photographs were taken at the request of the government. The first Hastings to land at Labuan was on 6th October; the aircraft en route Manila-Singapore developed radio faults, which were rectified by the Detachment. A new camp cinema, built by RAF personnel and having a seating capacity of sixty, was opened on the 26th. Aircraft worked were twenty-six military and sixty-three civilian

A survey flight was made by a Convair-240 aircraft of Garuda Indonesian Airlines, prior to a regular service from Jakarta to Manila, making a total of five scheduled airline landings at Labuan. Garuda operated eight of these modern twin engine, pressurised airliners.

November saw two unscheduled aircraft arrivals. A DC-3 of the Swiss Red Cross and a US Navy Beechcraft, Captain and Mrs Cold-Williams US Naval Attaché en route Djakarta-Manila, were entertained by the Detachment. KLM suspended their flights indefinitely. Six military and sixty civilian aircraft were worked.

Mr McCloud, Chief Electrical Officer, British North Borneo, visited regarding the proposed new power link between the two RAF power stations. A bay was selected, in collaboration with the local constabulary, for small arms training. Trial shoots were made with .303 and Bren gun.

On 10th December 1950 No 2463900 AC1 J.Y. Clark died while playing football. He is buried at the Kranji Military Cemetery in Singapore.

Unscheduled aircraft movements were all Dakotas, one from Manila returning the US Naval Attaché to Djakarta; a RAF aircraft carrying war correspondents from Manila, the other bringing Christmas catering from RAF Changi. The Detachment worked fifty-seven civilian and seven military aircraft.

The new Airport Hotel was opened with a champagne party on 14th December. Personnel attended a Christmas Draw and Dance at the Labuan Club on Christmas Eve. A Christmas Dinner with ten guests was held at the Airport Hotel on Christmas evening, followed by a dance. Numerous gifts were received from airlines, trading companies and residents, as well as a gift of $60 from local European residents. The gifts included four poultry dinners and twelve large bottles of beer per airman.

In January 1951 the first Valetta aircraft of 48 Squadron landed during a survey flight, which included landings at Kuching, Sandakan and Jesselton to confirm suitability for operation by these twin engine Vickers aircraft that were replacing the ubiquitous C-47 Dakota, also eventually equipping Nos 52 and 110 Squadrons in the Far East Air Force. The Valetta became affectionately known as the 'Pig' in RAF service because of its porcine silhouette when in flight.

Many aircraft companies worldwide sought to make a 'Dakota' replacement; most fell by the wayside and the Dakota lived on in service for many more years. By the mid-1950s the RNZAF started replacing their Dakotas with the Bristol Freighter in 41 Squadron, although retaining some Dakotas until 1977. The RAAF soldiered on with the Dakota until 1958 when their first C-130 Hercules came into Australian service.

Two DC-4 airliners of KLM refuelled during February, en route from Holland to Australia with 110 emigrants. An RAF Dakota from Jesselton to Changi brought Air Vice-Marshal R.S. Blucke CB, CBE, DSO, AFC on an inspection of the detachment and runway.

Later in the month four RAF Dakotas and three Sunderland aircraft, including DP 198, brought a detachment of 81 Squadron from Seletar. From February 1951 until September a Mosquito was regularly detached to Labuan. With the erection of tentage the unit strength was increased from seventeen to fifty, including RAAF Signals personnel.

A former customs shed was transferred to the power station to accommodate two cat diesel electric units. Piped water was provided to the squadron and photographic sections. During February the Unit worked seventy civilian and twenty military aircraft.

RNZAF Freighter NZ 5903. (Photo: Author)

In March 81 Squadron started another photographic survey; photographs of PF 672 and VL 615 clearly show that aircraft were still the parked on pierced steel planking (PSP) at this time. KLM continued staging their DC-4 emigration flights from Holland to Australia through Labuan.

A detachment of eight RAAF Signals personnel arrived, greeted by Wg Cdr Peters and Flt Lt Williams RAF from FEAF. Later in the month Gp Capt. Alexander RAAF of HQ RAAF inspected the camp, en route from Hong Kong to Australia. Total strength of RAF Labuan at 31st March was sixty-two; during the month the Detachment worked fifty-three military and seventy-eight civilian aircraft.

In April the non-scheduled and visiting aircraft comprised: 1st April KLM DC-4 from Holland to Australia with sixty migrants. A Short Solent flying boat for Trans Oceanic Airways (TOA), an Australian airline, alighted on a ferry flight UK to Australia.

4th April four D.H. Vampires of No 60 Squadron arrived en route from Singapore to Manila, via Labuan to demonstrate the aircraft in the Philippines; Dakota KN 301 flew as Air/Sea Rescue link, the aircraft departing on the 5th.

On the 8th two C-46 Commando aircraft of an American organisation called Civil Air Transport, (CAT), later known as Air America, staged through en route from Hong Kong to Australia.

On the 16th the Vampire flight returned from Manila and on the following day carried out local flying to show the flag over Jesselton, Seria and Brunei and then departed for Kuching. A D.H. Hornet and a Beaufighter staged through from UK to Hong Kong.

On the 20th a KLM DC-4 staged from Holland to West New Guinea, returning on the 23rd. On ANZAC Day, 25th April, the RAAF personnel paraded at the War Cemetery. A record total of sixty-six people were accommodated at the Unit and a further 121 RAF personnel stayed at the Airport Hotel. The Detachment worked 218 military and 166 civilian aircraft during the month, a new record.

June saw a USAF B-17 ASR aircraft pass through from Manila to Changi, returning later in the month. Other American aircraft included a DC-3 carrying the US Vice Consul of Singapore and a DC-3 carrying a medical team to Changi. RAF traffic included two Valettas, a Sunderland and a fully laden Hastings from Manila to Changi called to refuel.

KLM flew sixty migrants to Australia and returned three days later having come via West New Guinea. Garuda Indonesian Airways started scheduled flights using Convair aircraft in April 1951 flying Djakarta-Labuan-Manila on Thursdays, returning on Saturdays. Scheduled flights continued through Labuan by Malayan Airways, Qantas, Cathay Pacific and Shell Co, a total of sixty-eight aircraft per month.

The King's birthday was celebrated with a parade on the Padang. The Signals Detachment was augmented by 81 Squadron, RAAF, Royal Engineers and two visiting WRAF officers, Flt Officers Toyne and Thomas. The Labuan constabulary and auxiliary personnel also attended the parade, which was inspected by the Resident. Two Mosquito aircraft of 81 Squadron flew past and three cheers were given for His Majesty.

By September the runway was reported to be breaking up, and Air Headquarters were pursuing urgent repairs by the Director of Civil Aviation.

Sunderland RN 282, V of 209 Squadron arrived on 7th April 1952 on an anti-piracy patrol. Early in July Sqn Ldr Eames staged through in Sunderland SZ 566, Z, en route to Iwakuni, Japan as part of the United Nations Korean coast patrol force.

In October 1952 Labuan was included in a royal visit by the Duchess of Kent and her son to Kuching and North Borneo. The tour in a Sunderland was accompanied by two other Sunderlands carrying the support party and luggage.

The Coronation of Queen Elizabeth II was celebrated by RAF units around the world. Bill Kelley was a flight engineer on the Sunderlands of 209 Squadron based at Seletar and often visited Labuan. The most notable occasion was on Coronation Day, 2nd June 1953. The night before Sunderlands of 209, led by Sqn Ldr Eames VB 888, Bill's crew (RN 282 Flt Lt Arnaud; NJ 177 Flt Lt Clarke and DZ 566 Flt Lt Kingshott) flew to various places in what was then British North Borneo for the night.

Our crew with the CO on board went to Jesselton, which was the capital of BNB. On Coronation Day itself we all formed up and flew in formation all around BNB 'showing the flag' at these outposts of the Empire. That night we all ended up at Labuan where we had a rather splendid party in the Airport Hotel.

During 1954, 81 Squadron carried on attempting to complete the survey of Borneo with a detachment from 9th April until the end of the month. Of the twenty-eight sorties flown, involving eighty-six hours, only ten were successful. The June detachment had a very low success rate due to technical problems and the loss of an aircraft. On the 10th, Mosquito RG 268 had a defective undercarriage valve. The pilot Fg Off A.J. Knox burned off fuel for three hours before landing; the aircraft was written off, but both the pilot and navigator Fg Off A.B. Thompson were safe. This detachment covered 4000 square miles leaving 11,000 outstanding.

On his thirtieth birthday, 3rd July, Doug Allen, then a Flight Lieutenant, arrived at Labuan as OC the 81 Squadron detachment. In view of his birthday he gave his detachment a weekend off. He flew two surveys on the 5th in Mosquito RG 302, each of just over two hours, and one on the following day in the same aircraft with his usual navigator Fg Off Broom, this flight extending to five hours.

81 Squadron group. (Photo: D.G. Allen)

The 7th July was a busy day with a survey of three and three-quarter hours, followed by a piracy reconnaissance of the same duration. The six survey flights flown during the following week were all of at least four hours duration. During this week Doug carried out two single engine landing practices, two a month was normal practice, and two brief formation flights.

Doug returned again in July, memorable because of a very bad jellyfish bite which scarred his foot. During that detachment he met the Australian aircrew of World Wide Surveys. In August Anson VL 334 was used for one sortie.

In 1954 an Australian company, World Wide Surveys, bought two Mosquito PR41 aircraft, A52-306 (originally A52-197) and A52-313 (originally A52-204), which were re-registered as N 1596V and N 1597V. They were modified with fuselage cameras and contracted by US Army Map Services to carry out a survey of Borneo. On 9th June N1596V flew via Cloncurry and Darwin to Suarbaya, Indonesia where it was impounded as a spy plane and only released, after much diplomatic activity, to fly to Labuan. N1597V left Australia on 12th June and arrived at Labuan via Darwin and Sorong, which at that time was still part of the Netherlands East Indies. The survey was unsuccessful due to persistent bad weather and the two aircraft returned to Australia in September.

Throughout 1955 there was regular Sunderland traffic to and through Labuan; 88 Squadron had been disbanded in October 1954. The remaining Sunderlands at Seletar became 205/209 Squadron. Flt Lt Lockyer, EJ 155, flew General Sir Charles Loewen GCB, KBE, DSO, the CinC Far East Land Forces, on a tour of Borneo early in January, followed by PP 137 on anti-piracy patrol later in the month.

EJ 155 alighted at Labuan on several occasions during February. There were two separate Sunderland arrivals during March. In April Exercise Jungle Trek Patrol involved Sunderlands RN 278, Flt Lt Carroll; SZ 572, Flt Lt Innes-Smith; and RN 200 Flt Lt Dark in flights via Labuan to Sandakan and Lahad Batu.

There was a further anti-piracy patrol by Flt Lt Carroll, NJ 191, during May. Early in August the Squadron commander, Wg Cdr A.F. Fegen, flew the Colonial Secretary Mr Alan Lennox-Boyd and Lady Lennox-Boyd via Labuan, in the same aircraft, on a tour of British North Borneo.

In September Flt Lt Carroll, again in NJ 191, flew the AOC in C of FEAF Air Marshall Sir Francis Fressange KBE, CB, on a nine-day tour of Borneo.

Eddie Heywood wrote:

Arrived New Year's day 1956 at RAF Changi via the normal route a chartered York aircraft from UK through Pakistan/India/ Thailand. Just an eighteen year old RTDF operator and in awe of everything.

Soon I was told I was being detached to Labuan for nine months. I had heard mixed stories about the lack of nightlife, no opposite sex to speak of and general boredom.

Labuan of the fifties had a small population mainly in Victoria the only town and a few fishing villages scattered around the coasts. For someone from the industrial North of England seeing the miles of beautiful beaches with pristine sands and coral reefs teeming with fish was a wonder. Labuan had the only deep-water port in North Borneo, which was kept busy exporting the valuable timber.

The role of RAF Labuan was a re-fuelling staging post for RAF aircraft flying between Changi and Hong Kong and as the airfield closed at 18:00 hours (no runway lighting) it meant that unlike Changi, no nightshift work. The airfield was used by civilian aircraft too and it was interesting to see the various airlines visiting like Cathay Pacific, Garuda and a host of visitors from other Air forces. My particular favourite was the RAF Sunderland's visiting to refuel and alighting in the harbour.

In the fifties the camp had just three 16-man billets and the strength varied between 30 and forty airmen and NCOs. One billet housed mostly RAAF signals personnel who would not tell us what they did, but everyone knew anyway!!! These secretive Australians were replaced by RAF personnel belonging to 367 Signals Unit Hong Kong.

When off duty, swimming, badminton, football etc. ensured we were all pretty fit. The radio played a large part in our relaxation and I was introduced to Elvis, Holly and the Everley Brothers whilst in Labuan.

Treks into the jungle and boat trips to neighbouring islands ensured we were never bored. Labuan then, as now enjoyed duty-free status, so the evenings in the bar were cheap and cheerful.

Food was quite often a problem as our protein was ferried to us from Changi weekly and in the event an aircraft was faulty (which often happened) meant survival on hard rations, supplemented with local fish and fresh fruit. Our chef found that tinned corned beef could be served as hash, fritters and curried.

In fact Eddie spent virtually all of his first Far East tour in Labuan, marrying in September 1957 and returning to Changi in June 1958. Fifty years later he still has an affinity with the island and returns regularly.

In February Fg Off Kirkham flew a search operation from Labuan in Sunderland NJ 272 trying to find overdue vessel, the MV *Lee*, but the search proved to be unsuccessful.

Brian Roche sent a cutting by 'our air correspondent' (newspaper and date unknown):

40 AIRMEN 'EXILES' ON AN ISLAND

The RAF 'exiles' on Labuan are a happy breed of men.

Labuan 719 miles from Singapore, four flying hours in a Valetta of the Far East Transport Wing, is a valuable transport staging post and for this reason a detachment of the RAF is stationed there.

It is a small island and the total population is only 9,000, 3,000 are Chinese and the rest with the exception of 13 European and two Eurasian families and 300 Indians are either Malay or North Borneo Malay.

The RAF Unit is only 40 strong, consisting of one Officer – Flight Lieutenant J.B. 'Starry' Knight – three NCOs and 36 airmen. The tour of duty is one year for the officer and six months for the airmen.

Personally I should have described it as a rugged existence, and should not have been surprised if I had heard the expression 'Get me out of this' and 'Roll on the Boat'. But not a bit of it. Everyone I talked to was thoroughly happy and loud in their praises of the civilian population, who apparently go out of their way to make the airmen happy.

Sergeant A. Ironside, the Unit's cook, who joined the RAF in 1938 and who has served in Japan, Malaya, Europe and the Middle East has just completed two and a half years in Labuan and has asked for more.

L.A.C. A.A. Atkinson who comes from Birmingham is another with no fault to find. The only grouse I heard was that when the rains beat on the tin roof in Victoria, the noise is so loud that you can't hear the film, but he was quick to add that another cinema has just been built.

There is a cinema on the camp itself, an open sided building which bears the proud title of 'Her Majesty's'. The men's quarters are equally well named being Elizabeth and Sir Winston.

These airmen who have to deal with the arrival and departure of Vampires, Venoms, Yorks, Dakotas, Valettas, Canberras, Meteors and occasional visits from United States Air Force, still find plenty of time for sport.

They have two Dyak canoes and underwater fishing at a coral reef is very popular and they are experimenting with a homemade aqua-lung.

The airfield can hardly be described as a beauty spot but the exiles say that it might be much worse and that from an airman is praise indeed.

Brian Roche remembers: 'OC Troops during 1956–57 was one L/Cpl Toni Smith. One memory of Toni, which he considered to be his prime duty, was to give us Penguins proper range practice, with blow pipes 1, and darts 3 (non-toxic). One was awarded a marksman's badge for hitting a fag packet at 50 yards.'

Wg Cdr A.F. Fegen, ML 797, flew transport flights from Sandakan to Labuan and return in May 1956 and in the following month flew the Sultan of Brunei to Singapore via Labuan in Sunderland NJ 191.

During July Sqn Ldr J.W. Moffatt had a five-day familiarisation detachment of Borneo, based at Labuan in Sunderland SZ 577.

In September 1956 there were 490 movements reported, including the CinC French Navy. It was reported that on average there were two games of soccer per week, a game of rugby, and cricket. A dance was held at the Recreation Club and a barbeque on camp to celebrate and commemorate the Battle of Britain.

The Mosquito, which had flown its last sortie in the Far East in December 1955, had been replaced on 81 Squadron by the Meteor PR 10. VS 971, Flt Lt R.M. Brown, and VS 980, Fg Off N.J. Abbott flew to Clark Field via Labuan on 19th December, returning on 3rd January.

In January 1957 day tours were organised for airmen to visit the Seria oilfield installations, travelling in parties of eight in Shell Company's Prince aircraft. In May a new airport was opened at Brunei and the RAF carried out an air display as part of the ceremony. Sqn Ldr Cooper and Flt Lt Baff from 45 Squadron had set out the arrangements early in April. The full team of fifteen ground crew, a reserve pilot who was to carry out the commentary and an air traffic controller flew into Labuan in a Valetta of 52 Squadron and a Bristol Freighter of 41 Squadron RNZAF on 6th May. On the 7th the five DH Venom aircraft flew to Labuan and carried out a rehearsal for the full display. The runway at Brunei was not cleared for jet aircraft so the Venoms flew from Labuan for an eleven-minute display in front of the Sultan of Brunei, culminating in a 'bomb burst' which was followed by a solo display by Sqn Ldr Cooper, finishing with a high speed fly past by all five Venoms. The pilots were later flown to Brunei in the New Zealand Bristol 'Vibrator' as the Freighter was affectionately nicknamed, for an evening reception given by the Sultan. The detachment flew back to their base in Butterworth on 9th May via Kuching and Tengah.

During July three Scottish Aviation Twin Pioneer aircraft JZ-PPX; JZ-PPY; and JZ-PPZ ferried through from Saigon on delivery to de Kroonduif airline (a KLM subsidiary) to Sorong via Zamboanga.

Flt Lt Fenn, DP 198, carried out two anti-piracy patrols arriving on 17th November. John Feltham (Tich) wrote on RAF Forum about this visit:

> I only went there once on anti-piracy patrol with a Sunderland and spent two nights there. A corporal ran the bar in half a Nissen hut and it was only open for two hours a night. You were rationed to two half bottles of beer per man per day and twenty fags. The beer was San Miguel and did nothing for you after being used to Tiger.
>
> I remember the orderly Corporal, when he turned up to issue me my bedding was wearing KD Shorts, Working blue top, no socks and flip-flops and he was on duty, good lad. In the billet and the only other person in there was a heap of blankets on a bed that couldn't stop shivering, the lad was suffering from Malaria. Glad I was never posted there poor bu**ers.

Ian Edwards, then a sergeant signaller on that patrol, recalls when leaving Labuan on the 21st their low-flying airfield beat-up was reckoned by Air Traffic Control to be the lowest on record at an estimated six inches.

Two Hastings of 48 Squadron WD 490, Flt Lt J. Munro and WD498, Fl/Lt G.E. Wright carried out a troop lift to Sandakan via Labuan later in the month.

The Sunderland crews of 205/209 carried out two anti-piracy patrols during January 1958: Flt Lt Ford DFM, PP 127, followed four days later by Flt Lt Foster in RN 282. The Sunderland flying boat would be phased out and substituted by the Shackleton, the first Shackleton arriving on 1st January 1958.

On 3rd February Sunderland RN 282 flew to Labuan on a training flight. Early in March Flt Lt Bull and crew, RN 270, on anti-piracy, also searched for an Indonesian gunboat reported seen off the coast of Borneo.

On 17th March Hastings TG 580, Flt Lt R.T.D. Scott, staged en route to New Zealand via Darwin, returning from Darwin on 31st March and returning to Changi on 1st April. At the end of March Flt Lt S. Bowater, DP 198, operated from Labuan on a ship shadowing exercise.

On April 18th a Transport Command Hastings, en route to Darwin, had an engine repaired at Labuan. On the same day six USAF F86 Sabre aircraft flew from Labuan to Paya Lebar, being given cover by a Sunderland of 205/209. On the following day Hastings TG 520 staged through from Kai Tak to Changi.

In May Flt Lt Weaver, RN 270, carried out another anti-piracy patrol. On 16th June Wg Cdr MacReady, the new CO of 205/209 Squadron, with Flt Lt

Boutell, flew the first Shackleton, VP 254, into Labuan to check on airfield services and facilities, leaving on the following day. They returned in WB 854 in October to spend some time in discussing anti-piracy matters.

48 Squadron Hastings carried out a parachute drop on mainland Borneo on 2nd June. Two Hastings TG 586, Flt Lt Robinson and TG 520, Flt Lt Parfitt arrived on a Labuan special flight on 6th June.

Personal Memories

During the author's time at Labuan in 1958 the airfield was known as Labuan International.

Daily users of the airfield were Borneo Airways, based at Labuan and with their own hangar. There were three Scottish Aviation Twin Pioneers in service (VR OAD, VR OAE, and VR OAF) and two De Havilland Dragon Rapide biplanes.

D H Rapides and Twin Pioneer. (Photo: Author)

D H Rapide rebuild. (Photo: Author)

D H Rapide rebuild. (Photo: Author)

The DH Rapides (VR OAA had originally been NR 844 in RAF service; VR OAC was ex RAF having been NR 724) flew daily to Anduki, Lutong, and Sibu, returning via Lutong and Anduki to Labuan. There was a third Rapide being rebuilt. I asked the Australian chief engineer what was the problem. 'The ants just ate it.'

There were other regular users based elsewhere; the missionaries of the Borneo Evangelical Mission had an Auster J-5B VR WAA.

Borneo Evangelical Mission Auster J-5B. (Photo: Author)

Brunei Shell Petroleum Company operated Percival Prince aircraft, VR UDA, VR UDB, VR UDC and VR UDR, all of which were regular visitors

114

to Labuan; they also used three S-55 helicopters, one of which was VP BAF. These helicopters, chartered from World Wide Helicopters, were on floats.

Shell Aviation S-55 Helicopter. (Photo: Author)

Shell Aviation Percival Prince. (Photo: Author)

Malayan Airways flew from Singapore to Kuching and Sibu to Labuan and onward to Jesselton and Sandakan on a daily basis with DC-3. Initially these carried the Union flag above the registration on the fin, e.g. VR SCW, and later the Malay flag on VR RCP. Cathay Pacific staged through about once a week with DC-6 aircraft, VR-HFF being one example, en route Hong Kong to Kuching, and Garuda Indonesian came through from Djakarta to Manila with Convair-340s. We were not involved with these but they were interesting to see.

I had known of the island of Labuan from the time that my brother had been there on detachment in the 1940s with 81 Squadron, but had given it little thought. While at RAF Seletar in 1958 I was told about an article in one of the English papers. The *People* Sunday newspaper had a regular feature by Arthur Helliwell called 'The Man of the People'. He had been given a flight to the Far East and published a few articles; in one he expressed disgust at cockfighting under the Union Jack at Labuan in Borneo. One of his interviews featured Eifon Evans, one of our corporals, who was on detachment on the island of Labuan.

In July I had been called to see our squadron leader, a big bluff Derbyshire man. Running the squadron orderly room was Sergeant 'Abble Dabble' Woolons, who I had known on 51 MT in Egypt. I realised I was wanted elsewhere; the OC was reluctant to let me go but initially could not make much sense of the phone call taking place. At one point I realised that someone was confusing me with my namesake, as he replied, 'No no no, this one is a bloody good bloke.' High praise indeed. During the phone call Abble Dabble came in with a signal and, just to keep me amused, scrunched it up and ate some imaginary fish and chips out of it.

The squadron leader lost, and the upshot was that on 21st July 1958 I was to be detached to RAF Changi for duty at Labuan to replace Eifon. There were very few single corporals in my trade in the Far East and the Command drafters had forgotten that Eifon was due home.

The Chinese civilian fitters on the engine production line were convinced that I would be surrounded by bare-breasted maidens and seemed to envy me. My mother was worried when she got my letter; following trouble in the Middle East the US Marines had gone into Lebanon and she got the two confused. I had a couple of quiet evening drinks at Changi transit and a fitful night's sleep. I had no idea how long I would be away; six months would be normal for a detachment, but no time had been specified.

There was much shuffling of lists when I boarded the Valetta; I was a last-minute passenger on a routine flight bound for Hong Kong. There was an urn of squash lashed to a bench and everybody, except me, had a packed lunch box to last them until their night stop at the American base Clark Field in the Philippines.

Sometime after take-off, the aircraft captain came around and scrounged a sandwich here and an apple there to make up a box for me. I thought it was most kind and I finished up with a better box than anyone else. I guess the flight took about four hours; we crossed a stretch of the South China Sea and then flew in sight of the Sarawak coast.

The Valetta flew the Hong Kong route via Labuan, which was just a staging post, Clark Field for a night stop and then into Kai Tak, Hong Kong. Should they be unable to land at Kai Tak they could return to Clark Field. On the return flight to Changi they staged anticlockwise around the South China Sea via Saigon.

Eifon was glad to see me and picked me up in the Land Rover, although the detachment huts were only a few yards from the aircraft pan. Until a few people left there was no bed for me. Ted the sergeant chef who was doing the whole of a two and a half year unaccompanied tour at Labuan was on leave in Penang so I used his bunk.

Malayan Airways DC-3. (Photo: Author)

Garuda Convair 340 PK-GCM. (Photo: Author)

Cathay Pacific DC-4 VR-HFF. (Photo: Author)

I met the Detachment OC, our sole officer. Jack a flight lieutenant pilot, had served in Italy; he wore a couple of WWII ribbons and the Queen's Commendation. He had apparently flown fighters but not a lot was known about him.

Eifon wasted no time in showing me around and handing over everything on his charge. On a normal unit only senior NCOs and officers held inventories but Labuan was an exception, I found to my surprise that even the RAF ensign was mine. The other surprise was to realise that I had not driven for almost eighteen months.

The most important thing to learn was how to load the Leyland 2500-gallon bowser, as none of the three SAC drivers were qualified to drive or operate it. Avtur fuel arrived by sea at the Shell Agency, on the coast just outside the town, in 45-gallon drums. These drums had to be manhandled and upended at the back of the truck, then via a suction hose and stand pipe they were self-loaded by the vehicle through a big streamline filter trolley. It was bloody hard work as it took fifty-three drums to fill the tank, and the pump sucked it almost as fast as the next drum could be stood up, opened and the empty rolled away. It proved to be a good muscle-building exercise.

81 Squadron Meteor PR10. (Photo: Author)

Eifon assured me that very few turbine aircraft called, the 81 Squadron Meteor PR 10 then on the pan being an exception. The MT were only responsible for refuelling gas turbine aircraft as the airfield had a hydrant system for high octane AVGAS that the older piston-engined aircraft used. Little did I know that I was going to see some very busy periods on the detachment, but as nothing compared to the Brunei revolt and Indonesian Confrontation later in the 1960s.

The Detachment had two functions, principally as a staging post. A group of corporals and J/Ts, one of each aircraft trade, had the important task of seeing the visiting aircraft safely through. The normal route was to Hong Kong, via Clark Field in the Philippines. The route from the UK for Transport Command at that time was very devious: following the Suez action they could not fly over the Middle East, so aircraft were routed down to West Africa and across Central Africa to Aden, Bahrain, Gan and Singapore. The RAF could not over fly Indonesia due to an ongoing rebellion, aircraft from Singapore to Australia invariably staged via Labuan.

There were various Hastings transients, an Australian special on 21st July and WD 498 to Darwin on the following day. One of these ignored the

119

Valetta. (Photo: Author)

Hastings TG 557. (Photo: Author)

batsman signals while taxiing in, so the corporal in charge of marshalling dropped the bats and walked away. This caused a row but the pan was of an awkward shape and if the aircraft was not turned quickly enough it could not taxi out. We tried to tow the aircraft back to a better position with the Land Rover and the Bedford RL truck. The tow bar jaws kept releasing until several layers of paint were scraped off showing settings for such WW2 aircraft as Oxford and Wellington. After adjustment we moved it far enough to proceed.

Valetta en route to Hong Kong still called, but this route was gradually taken over by the Hastings of 48 Squadron based at Changi. We had a

Hastings. (Photo: Author)

regular LAB-P flight on Tuesdays bringing in supplies, flown by either Valetta or Bristol Freighters of 41 Squadron RNZAF. The other important function was the signals listening post, a detachment of 367 Signals Unit, which crosschecked Chinese signals activities with units in Hong Kong. At that time the signals people were all airmen under a young sergeant. The sergeants were Ted the chef, 'Dusty' Rhodes i/c radio workshops and 'Tiger' Tyson, a Plymouth man, who was i/c stores and air movements; all of the rest of the sections were run by corporals.

RAF detachment. (Photo: Author)

Our hutted detachment was just off the airfield pan; the huts were named Elizabeth, Sir Winston, and Tensing, presumably built post-Coronation. They were comfortable, being five degrees north of the Equator and

121

offshore the climate was less humid than Singapore, but we slept in mosquito nets and had to take our daily Paludrine tablets.

The food was excellent. Our mess had a servery at one end and through folding doors was the bar. At breakfast we enjoyed the luxury of deciding how we wanted our eggs. We had a cooked lunch and, because we had no NAAFI, had a small buffet meal available at cease work, about four o'clock, which using our fluent Malay we called '*kitchi makan*'. We had an evening meal at about half past six or seven. I had had no cause to learn Malay in Singapore but now learned a little from the sign at the end of the runway, *Awas Kepalterbang Rendah* – beware low flying aircraft.

Each section had a pet dog and these would queue on the balcony each night to be fed; bones thrown out of the open doors to them never touched the floor and with one exception all of the dogs were well behaved. Fred, the MT dog, was built like a slim Labrador, and was whitish/cream in colour; he liked to scrounge a ride to the signals site in the hope of a feed.

The fire section boss was 'Taff' Hutchinson. He had a Land Rover crash rescue vehicle, an old Bedford OX water bowser and two new Thornycroft Dual Purpose Mk 1 fire tenders (DP). This was my first experience of the DPs; the Mk 1 was 4 × 4, and a good beast with a Rolls-Royce B80 engine and good water and foam compound tanks. When we unloaded the second one, which had come as deck cargo via Thailand, we were told that someone had tried to smuggle drugs in the fire equipment lockers. Two Land Rovers, the general hack and the OCs, a Bedford RL three-tonner, an Austin K9 one-ton 4 × 4 truck and an ambulance on a K9 chassis, initially only one Leyland 2500 refueller, made up the MT Section.

There were one fitter and three drivers, who took it in turns to man the ambulance during flying with the sole medical orderly; they ferried the marine craft blokes to the quay or the football team to town. The signals shift changes were taken to and from the site at the other side of the airfield; during daylight the Land Rover's cloud of dust could be seen at a distance.

The evening signals shift took food with them and had a meal at midnight, and prepared a meal for the oncoming shift so the driver always had big eats on the late change. On the odd occasion that I helped out on this run I enjoyed home-cooked egg and chips very much.

RAF Changi parented the detachment and all of my MT paperwork, which accounted for every mile and every gallon of petrol, was returned monthly. My predecessor had not let anyone touch any forms; everything was pristine, but bore little relation to actual fact. I made everyone do their own and they soon got used to it.

In usual RAF fashion the MT Officer at Changi was the last to know that another Seletar interloper was running his MT. Soon after my arrival I had a flying visit from a very pleasant Welsh squadron leader who came to look me over. I appeared to have impressed him until just before he got back on the aircraft when I told him not to worry as I could cope.

'Cope? Cope? I don't want you to cope, I want you to manage.'

To add insult to injury I could not find my beret to salute him on his way.

Shortly after, I had a visit from a staff officer from Headquarters Far East Air Force to check up on the MT. I had to point out to him that if any pressure refuelled aircraft came through I had no equipment to refuel them; in fairness the RAF had none of these aircraft based in the Far East at that time. He seemed surprised: 'Why not?' he asked, as if it was my fault. He must have got his finger out as I received a 2500-gallon dual purpose Leyland by sea fairly soon afterwards.

M T barn. (Photo: Author)

The vehicles were parked under Dutch barn type buildings quite near the domestic site and the tanker had stood near the airman's mess, I decided to move it away from the billets and nearer the pan, and cut a hard standing, big enough for both refuellers, out of the very coarse grass. Mike Choy our resident Air Ministry Works and Bricks bloke, an electrician by trade, had two Allen scythes so I used one of these and was most impressed that the apparently crude and heavy machine did such a good job.

The vehicle fleet was not a big problem. Harry left an oil filter loose once and those of us riding back with the football team were nearly choked as oil burnt on the exhaust pipe. The run up the hill from Victoria was interesting in the Austin: the engine temperature gauge was immediately in front of the driver and it was wise to drive by the temperature and not by the speedo.

The old water tanker sprang a leak from a core plug. British industry ensured that core plugs could be plugged with a two-shilling piece or a half crown as an emergency repair, but a dollar bill would not do the trick. This plug, behind the bell housing, was not in stock in the Far East, and when it arrived several weeks later Taff was helping to fight a scrub fire that threatened Victoria. We flogged on and by late afternoon had finished. The truck had not moved for a couple of months and driving away, the gear lever broke off. Duly repaired, the tanker was taken to Taff who said that he did not need the bloody old thing.

The telephone system, rarely used, hardly ever went wrong. It was the responsibility of a lance corporal of the Royal Signals; because he was the only pongo we called him OC Troops, or 'Troops' for short. He was on the unit on an indefinite basis and rebuilt, maintained and ran our cinema. Ken, one of the drivers, helped him and did more there than he did in the MT. I could only remember him as 'Troops', but found out fifty years afterwards that he was Michael Snowling, a Norfolk lad, serving under the name of Bartrum with the nickname of Sam. I told him that, a few years after he left, the post of Troops was upgraded to Major General.

Michael regularly gave film shows for children from the nearby St Anthony's School orphanage. Fr Bill Smit had taken over in 1948, describing his charges as war orphans; by the time he left in 1956 the orphanage had expanded, accommodating fifty-two boy orphans from Borneo, Brunei and Sarawak. Fr Martin Walsh followed and it was with Fr Walsh that Michael had most dealings.

Orphans' cinema show. (Photo: Michael Snowling)

Michael organised gifts for the boys, deciding to give them what they wanted, rather than what Fr Walsh hoped they would have. Fr Walsh was at this time struggling to make ends meet and fed the boys on just a few cents a day. Michael decided that rather than donate practical items he would leave that to the good father and let the boys have some toys. Most opted for toy boats, cars, trains and helicopters, or more practical table tennis, torch, wallet or fountain pens. Two asked for a sheath knife and others for toy guns. Four girls asked for dolls.

Michael still has letters from those days, variously to Dear Troops, expressing sadness at Michael's departure from Labuan. A later one to Uncle Mike from Vincent thanked him for the RAF books. Michael donated toy guns in 1959 and had a reply telling him what fun they would have playing cowboys. When he visited as a tourist in 1985, he was about to be introduced to the Reverend Mother when she recognised him and said, 'You are Troops!' He was almost overcome that she had remembered and recognised him.

Films for the detachment arrived courtesy of Malayan Airways or RAF airfreight. We received 'High Society' and it was decided to invite some of the local notabilities, 'Wheels' in then-current parlance, to a Borneo Premiere. It felt civilised to be in the company of European women, but Harry the fitter spoiled it by greeting the appearance of Grace Kelly in his thick Brummie accent: 'Oo it's Grice Killy the titless wunder.'

The bar opened for a short while at midday and from about eight to half ten at night. There were extended bar hours at weekends and special occasions. Corporals took it in turn to run the bar and made about 5 cents on each drink. After breakfast the big fridge was filled to ensure that cool beer would be available at lunchtime and that it would be cold by evening. Occasionally one would be put in the small freezer slot but if it was in too long it would freeze after being poured. One of the aerial erectors came in one lunch time and declared that he had never been hotter. He asked for the coldest beer in the house and to everybody's amusement, except his, he only got a glass of ice.

The bar also sold soap and toiletries; everyone used a talcum powder in that humid climate, and the only one stocked was prickly heat powder. A visiting air crewman complained one night that, having left his normal baby powder in his married quarter in Changi, he lay back and applied the prickly heat powder to his nether portions and nearly took off.

The Marine craft section, staffed by two corporals, a fitter and a coxswain, existed to ensure safe alighting and refuelling facilities for Sunderland flying boat movements, and consequently were not very busy. There was a marine tender powered by a Ford Parsons V8 and in lieu of a refuelling tender a bomb scow, from the hold of which they hand-pumped Avgas as and when needed; this was powered by two small Meadows petrol engines. Items such as u/s valves from the radios and heavy u/s spares that were uneconomic to return by air had to be certified as sea dumped, which was quite fun. I once took the tiller on the way back into the quay and learned to keep the bow pointing at a kampong down the coast in order to maintain the correct course for Small Ships quay.

I once took the ambulance down to the quay to watch a Sunderland alight and then went to the barbers to have my first haircut for several months. The OC sent someone to find me as a visiting Pembroke was coming back in with a problem. I watched him land safely and then went back to the barbers to finish the other half of my haircut. It was not often that we had an aircraft return, but an Aussie-bound Hastings came back in one day as the oil tank filler cap was insecure and a lot of oil had been lost before he landed.

A good mate was Fred (Ginger) Jones who was i/c the radio shack, a good source of information; we always knew the sex and status of visiting or transient passengers. On this depended the number of people who greeted the incoming aircraft. The US Ambassador and entourage came through in his personal DC-3 from Bangkok en route to Manila to do some shopping and stayed the night; we joined them at night for a drink.

The runway at Kai Tak had been extended by infilling the sea at the end of the runway and it was due to be officially opened. Two DH Venom fighters from RAF Tengah that were nearly time-expired were sent to give a

D H Venom. (Photo: Author)

Avro Shackleton. (Photo: Author)

flying display and then to be left in Hong Kong. These flew via Labuan with an escorting Shackleton (C of 205/209 Squadron) for Air Sea Rescue cover and an Australian Canberra A84-238 for navigational assistance. They stopped for the night and it was decided to give them some recreation during the afternoon, so together with the marine fitter we took them out around the harbour in the bomb scow. The hold boards were taken off and lashed to the stern in a crude attempt for these guys to try water skiing. One of the engines cut and the fitter gave me the tiller while he stuck his head in the engine space to rectify matters. I heard one of the pilots say, 'I hope this guy is OK on his asymmetric.' They left the following day, once I had refuelled my only Venoms and the first of many Canberras.

We were sitting quietly one Sunday when we were warned of an emergency landing of a Hercules. I had read of the first one that had visited Boscombe Down in 1956 but this was the first that I had seen. America had deployed forces from the US because of the Communist Chinese threat to the Quemoy islands. A pair of C-130s were over flying en route to Singapore with top brass on board. One Hercules had lost the use of an engine and, as the early aircraft were very marginal on safety with that engine out, they landed and the general transferred to the good aircraft.

On the following morning two aircraft flew in a staff sergeant with a lorry-mounted crane and spare engine, and left him to get on with it. He impressed me; having heard from our ex-Halton fitters about low American skill levels and the multiplicity of tradesmen that the USAF needed to do the simplest of jobs, it was good to see this guy quietly tackle the job single handed, finish the job and run the engine up. By the middle of the week he

127

was gone and we saw them no more. It was more than thirty years later before the RAF got an air-transportable crane.

USAF C 130 Hercules 50003. (Photo: Author)

USAF C 130 Herules 50512. (Photo: Author)

We talked to some of the Hercules crew; they had been involved in training the Royal Australian Air Force crews then converting to Hercules. The Americans were most patronising and were surprised how well the Aussies managed to absorb the training; I could not believe what I was hearing.

A passenger boat from nearby Brunei en route to Labuan went missing and a visiting Devon aircraft searched for it. I asked Jack if I could go as a

USAF C 130 Hercules engine change. (Photo: Author)

spare pair of eyes but he sent the coxswain instead. No trace of boat or bodies was found.

We had no NAAFI but had a block membership of the local club paid for by the RAF. This was quite civilised and made a pleasant change from time to time. Jack the OC was always keen to impress the 'Wheels', as the important civilians were nicknamed. These were a very varied group of people: English, Scots Australian, Indian, Eurasian and Chinese. There was an Australian in public works (PWD) who had won a Silver Star from the Americans in the South West Pacific theatre. He had surveyed a valley for an airstrip while fighting went on either side of him and over his head.

It was decided that we should join them on Papan, a nearby deserted island, for a barbecue one Sunday. Our OC was fanatical about not allowing flip-flops; consequently we wore socks at all times, but on this trip the flip-flops came into use and we all suffered agonies of sunburnt feet because we were no longer acclimatised.

Victoria town was a mixture of modern buildings in the centre and older local-style large huts on the outskirts. I visited the Chinese newsagent to ensure that I got my *Time* magazine on schedule. Like most Chinese he had difficulty in pronouncing 'Corporal', and all of the Borneo Airways pilots titled themselves 'Captain', so thereafter I was Captain Bale, which made our blokes laugh but made it a lot easier for the old boy. I snapped up some jazz records that he had in stock and he told me that he would order more if I could explain what jazz music was – that wasn't easy.

I found *Time* magazine to be excellent in its coverage of the by-election at home where Mark Bonham-Carter took the seat for the Liberals in a historic victory; it even seemed to get the Devon accent right in their reports.

The Chinese-owned cold store which provided most of our food also had a bar, which was useful for a couple of beers while the football team were down town playing. We would occasionally see a former district officer, now retired and living locally, having a drink with his young woman; it was said that he changed them every few years.

58 Squadron Canberra PR. (Photo: Author)

We had a detachment of PR Canberras from 58 Squadron who did a few weeks' photo reconnaissance; it was interesting to see them return with completed film, which went back to Singapore for processing on the next flight. The Canberra main tanks were filled after flight but the tip tanks had to be filled shortly before take-off; this meant an early start. While never feeling dawn was as exotic as described by Roger Annett in his excellent book *Drop Zone Borneo* I used to enjoy these mornings, as Mount Kinabulu and its adjoining range of mountains could be seen against the sunrise.

RAF Upwood used to send Canberras to the Woomera range in Australia from time to time. I saw one off early one morning and was asked by a supernumerary squadron leader what those blue things were on the horizon; I had to tell him that they were mountains.

The Dutch still had a toehold in the Far East; their navy used Martin Mariner amphibian aircraft, which used to be flown from Dutch New Guinea to Holland for major servicing. They used to stage via Labuan and on to Singapore to avoid Indonesian airspace. It was a massive aircraft powered by two 1700-hp radial engines; the bomb bay was behind the engine within the same nacelle.

Martin Mariner RNN Aviation Service. (Photo: Author)

Grumman Albatross. (Photo: Author)

Another amphibian that was a regular visitor was the Grumman Albatross, usually en route Manila to Singapore. Although our runway was adequate, one of these made a very short rocket assisted take-off to impress the natives.

The US Naval attaché to Thailand was an interesting bloke; he was returning to the States in a Beech-18 (US Navy SNB-1 39910) and claimed that a couple of his stages were a bit longer than his range.

We also saw Douglas C-54 of the US Air Force on a couple of occasions. I tried to take a photo of every visitor but did not always succeed.

The main workhorse of all of the nearby air forces was still the C-47 Dakota. A Philippine C-47 staged through from Indonesia with returned POWs from some unknown conflict; they sheltered under the wing having a

U S Navy Beech SNB-5. (Photo: Author)

U S Navy Beech SNB-5. (Photo: Author)

U S A F C-54. (Photo: Author)

U S A F C-54. (Photo: Author)

smoke while it was refuelled. I missed a shot of that, and also of a South Vietnamese C-47. Where this was going to or coming from I am not sure; it was supposedly before any formal help from the US, but these people spoke fair American and had US-style uniform.

The US Marines came through with a Super DC-3 (R4D-8); it was quite a different looking aircraft. I happened to be cycling back past the end of the runway when it landed and it was probably the worst couple of landings I've seen. Without doubt the best airmanship to be seen was Flying Officer P.P. Ashford-Smith, flying Valetta WD 167 calibrating the various radio airfield aids. When he had finished on one bearing he would heel around in a tight turn and line up for the next – it was most impressive.

One of the RAF's remaining Dakota voice aircraft 'HOPE' staged through following a major refurbish at Hong Kong; we also saw some civilian Dakotas from Caltex and Ansett.

RAAF C-47 A65 124. (Photo: Author)

Malayan Airways VR-SCW. (Photo: Author)

During 1958, 205/209 Squadron were in the course of converting from the Sunderland flying boat to the Avro Shackleton, a land-based maritime patrol aircraft. On 6th October Flt Lt Ford in Sunderland RN 303 arrived to carry out what proved to be the last anti-piracy patrol by a flying boat, returning to Seletar on 10th October. On the 17th Flt Lt Elias in Shackleton WB 854 flew in on a navigation exercise.

We heard that Jack had to go back to UK. We had a relief OC for a week or so who was rumoured to be under some sort of cloud and who decided to go back to Singapore via Hong Kong. I was helping to unload the LAB P (our supply aircraft) Valetta one Tuesday morning when the captain asked

Ansett Airways. (Photo: Author)

U S Navy R4D-8. (Photo: Author)

RAAF C-47 A65 94. (Photo: Author)

RAAF C-47. (Photo: Author)

RAF Dakota KJ 955. (Photo: Author)

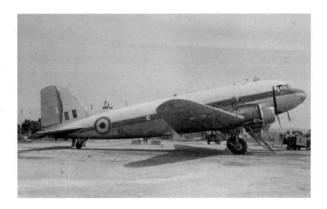

RAF Dakota KP 277. (Photo: Author)

U S Navy R4D-8. (Photo: Author)

U S Marine Corps R4D-8. (Photo: Author)

'where the bastard [flight lieutenant by name] was' as he had been 'covering for him at Changi'. I had to tell him he went thataway.

Jack handed over to Mike Fleetwood, a navigator from one of the Valetta squadrons, who proved to be as good an officer as we could have wished. Jack had left some paperwork unsigned and when I tried to get him to sort it before leaving he declined. As he drove away I heard him tell Mike, 'Good NCO that but inclined to be a bit dogmatic,' which I took as a compliment.

A Royal New Zealand Navy frigate HMNZS *Rotoiti* was due to call and had asked for several teams to be turned out. We found thirteen on the detachment who had played rugby at some time, and persuaded Mike Choy to play in the front row, his assistant, an Asian Games sprinter on the wing, and one of the 'Wheels' a Scottish bank manager at full back. The rudiments of the game were explained to the novices and we were as ready as would ever be. We played on the padang. A CPO was ref and trainer and asked me if they could play a couple of subs as they were desperate for a run; I had to decline. We played our hearts out. The front row battle was helped by Mike Choy's exotic breath, as the Kiwis whinged about it every time a scrum went down. I played wing forward; we were beaten 64-0. I was shattered and we had retired to the Chinese bar for a beer or two when we were summoned to the club to meet the District Officer. He was a Cornishman, Pascoe by name. He congratulated me and asked if I had played for St Lukes, which made me proud, and to feel that I had really pulled my weight. The Chinese middle school beat them at basketball but that apart they won everything else.

The Kiwis stayed for a couple of days and we gave them some hospitality and had a good few drinks with them at our place. I was called late one evening to the OC's room where after a few drinks they would not take no for an answer. I was sent to the ship and brought back their CO, who got them moving and said that he had left somebody in every port in the Far East so far and he was not going to do so at Labuan. This was Jack's farewell performance and things then settled down to a smoother routine.

Other visitors then were literally from another time and place. The Australians were allowing in a shipload of White Russians who had spent years in Hong Kong as stateless persons. Their ship stayed for several days and, over several drinks, we tried to introduce them to Aussie slang that they would need in their new home.

An air vice marshal called for a day; I never discovered the reason but after he left I posted a super full set of British North Borneo stamps that he had self-addressed for his collection.

We next heard that an Aussie Sabre squadron would stage through to their new base at Butterworth, which the Australians' airfield construction branch had refurbished. Operation Sabre Ferry started at the end of October 1958 with aircraft of No 3 Squadron RAAF coming through in flights of four aircraft. They flew via Darwin, Biak a KLM airfield on Mokmer Island then in Netherlands New Guinea (now Irian Jaya), Guiuan in the Philippines, with Zamboanga available as an alternative. 3 Squadron's history (*Secrets Revealed*) reports that the Americans from Clark Field had flown in graders and virtually reconstructed the ex-wartime airstrip Guiuan, and provided a mobile control tower and mobile canteens. They had high-level cover by Canberra A84-240 and had Neptune aircraft at strategic points. A couple of tradesmen had been attached ahead of the move so we saw a few Dakotas, which the Aussies still called 'Goony Birds'. The complete squadron move needed seven Dakotas. RAF Shackletons of 205 squadron carried out cover patrols on the route to Butterworth. Another visitor during Sabre Ferry was an Australian minister who travelled in his VIP Convair 440 Metropolitan

We indoctrinated the Aussies in our method of filling the refueller; in 1997 at the Australian fighter base museum 'Fighterworld' in Williamtown NSW I met a retired RAAF attendant who had accompanied one of the Canberras, and he remembered Labuan for the refuelling alone.

No 3 Squadron had fought in the Middle East and Italy during the Second World War equipped with Gladiators, Hurricanes, Kittyhawks and finally Mustangs. The CAC Sabre was an interesting aircraft with a Rolls Royce Avon engine and two Aden cannon in place of the .5 machine-guns fitted by the Americans. Refuelling was by open line and we sent them on their way, having taken several photos.

One Sunday, following a good lunch, a group of us decided to get on to 'Brodies' beach and walk around the coast of the island. We went for some distance quite easily, passing the Membedai, Shell Oil's rest house hotel, and came across some aircraft remains. We thought that they might have been Jap or possibly Kittyhawks, and for years among my souvenirs I had the encrusted remains of a spark plug. We then came to a low cliff which we had to round in water of uncertain depth. Eccles was selected to be first in the water and we took the mickey at his caution and laughed even more when the water turned out to be only a couple of feet deep.

When we reached a beach by a small kampong we felt that teatime was calling and that we had better head back. A young lad approached and we tried our Malay on him: *jalan* was street or travel and *kepalterbang* was aircraft. We thought '*Syah piggi jalan kepalterbang*' would have been 'I want the road to

3 Sqdn RAAF CAC Sabre A94-956. (Photo: Author)

3 Sqdn RAAF CAC Sabre A94-955. (Photo: Author)

General Sabreferry scene. (Photo: Author)

Air Minister's Convair 440. (Photo: Author)

aircraft'. He nodded and shinned up the nearest tree and threw us down two coconuts. We trusted to instinct and were back on camp before dark.

On Sundays we would sometimes cycle to a nearby kampong to watch the local sports of cockfighting and top spinning competitions. There was a small arena laid out where cocks would be matched one against the other – not a pretty sight. The tops were spun and then picked up to run on a large piece of glass; the winner was the top that spun the longest.

One of the RAF vehicles was hit by a Fiat 500 driven by the company secretary of Borneo Airways, who had a drink taken. Rumour had it that the police chief had no time for that group of 'Wheels' and was determined to clobber him. I explained to the driver how to make out his couple of dozen accident forms, RAF Form FMT 3, the format of which was the best accident prevention lesson ever devised. Several copies were required and I went to each vehicle to try to find enough, with no luck. The OC signalled Changi for 200 copies and on the next aircraft a Flight Sergeant arrived to find out how many accidents we'd had. The matter eventually came to court and I had to attend. My KD shirts were rotten; none were available from Changi or locally so I borrowed one from Ginger. The magistrate looked comical as he came into court in shorts, but only his jacket and tie were visible over the desk.

Even on a small detachment like Labuan we could not expect to get away without an AOC's inspection. This was to be done by Air Vice Marshal Hancock, RAAF, who was the AOC 224 Group. During the Confrontation he was to visit Labuan again as the Chief of Air Staff of the RAAF. Ted the Sergeant Chef, who had not done a parade for nearly twenty years volunteered to be NCO i/c, to everybody's surprise. I was excused, as I had to drive the old Land Rover as baggage wagon. Ted, who had a massive waist, volunteered to blanco his own webbing belt.

AOC's Parade. (Photo: Author)

They greeted the old man smartly as he stood by his Pembroke and I took a few photos. He gave us no aggravation, but thought that the Austin ambulance should have been air-conditioned. When the photos were printed it was discovered that Ted had forgotten to wear his webbing belt.

The Sunderland made what we were told would be its farewell visit to Labuan and I went out in the tender to get some photos as DP 198 (W), one of the 'boats' built on Lake Windermere, alighted, and on the following day it made a very low pass over the airfield.

Shackleton Loss: A Diary

Monday 8th December 1958

In December 1958 a Shackleton VP254, B of 205 Squadron from Changi, arrived to carry out an anti-piracy patrol, a problem then and now. Questions about local piracy were still being asked in the House of Commons in 1963 and there have been many more reports since the millennium. The crew stopped the night at the Airport Hotel. I happened to be i/c the bar that week and saw some of them before they went to see the lights and sights of Victoria. They called in for a nightcap on their return. The flight engineer took delight in trying to get the young Chinese lady on the telephone exchange to find out the Brisbane Test match score; it caused quite a bit of amusement.

Shackleton VP 254 8 December 1958. (Photo: K. Martin)

I did not know, until fifty years later at the memorial service, that ground crew had flown in to service the aircraft for the duration of the detachment at Labuan. They were F/O Clements, Cpl Everett, George Gatcum, radio fitter, J/T Alastair McLean, and SAC Hawes. They had been offered a flight to act as extra observers, but luckily for them they had declined.

This aircraft had first flown on 28th March 1950 but remained at Woodford until 1954, was transferred to Langar in December 1954 and prepared for IFF Mk10 and SARAH, was used at Boscombe Down and returned to the Air Ministry in January 1958 and allotted to 205 Squadron in May.

Tuesday 9th

On the Tuesday morning the Shackleton took off on an anti-piracy patrol with a full crew:

Flt Lt W.A.S. Boutell, Pilot	F/Sgt D. H.G.N. Dancy DFC, Flight Engineer
Flt Lt S. Bowater DFC AFC, Co-Pilot	F/Sgt E.L. Owen ⎫
Flt Lt A.C. Moore, Navigator	Sgt P.C. Barnley ⎬ Signallers
Fg Off M.A.C. Jones, Navigator	Sgt P. Marshall ⎪
Master Signaller J. Stewart	Sgt J.E. Sixsmith ⎭

Mr A.R. Miller the Acting Deputy Police Commissioner was on board as part of the anti-piracy patrol.

Flt Lt S. Bowater had flown Sunderland flying boats for many years and had been converting to the Shackleton; he flew this sortie as co-pilot, standing in for a colleague convalescing from appendicitis. He had been awarded the DFC while flying with No 101 Squadron on Airborne Cigar countermeasures operations in 1944 and the Air Force Cross (AFC) while flying in relief of the North Greenland Expedition with No 230 Squadron in 1955.

F/Sgt D.H.G.N. Dancy had been awarded the DFC while a warrant officer with XV squadron in 1945.

Ginger Jones, my mate in charge of the W/T shed, told me at lunchtime that they had been diverted to check on an American merchant ship that had hit a reef. This was later said to be an adventure trip schooner the *Ian Crouch*.

Signals from the aircraft presented for the subsequent Board of Enquiry give brief details:

Eleven survivors sighted [these were fishermen from Taiwan].

32 minutes later; of trying to attract the attention of a ship fifteen nautical miles west of the island.

This ship was reported as five miles away from thirteen survivors, who were flying the Nationalist Chinese flag.

The Shackleton was ordered to take photos of the rescue ship, the photos were confirmed and stated to be 'flush deck clipper bow diesel powered fishing boat 110 feet and 120 tons. Registered number YF 890'. Ordered to stand by until the rescue was complete the survivors were reported to be salvaging equipment.

Questioned about the arrival of the rescue ship, the Shackleton reply estimated that rescue would be complete within twenty minutes, but there was no communication with the ship. Orders were given to continue the anti-piracy patrol when the rescue was completed and land at Labuan before dark.

The final message from the Shackleton stated 'USAF B 29 arrived'. Nothing further was heard. Later in the day we were told that contact had been lost with the aircraft and that a search would be started at first light.

Wednesday 10th

Fg Off Ken Appleford AFC, in 205 Squadron Shackleton WB 827 based at RAF Changi, Singapore, had taken off at midnight on the 9th for the six-hour flight, which would bring him to the last known position as dawn was breaking. There they spotted a vessel similar to that previously reported, but could not make radio contact with it and the crew onboard made no attempt to contact them.

No trace of wreckage could be seen; neither were any survivors sighted so they widened their search area. Finally, after being airborne for over sixteen hours, Ken landed his aircraft at Labuan. For five days Ken and his crew searched an ever-widening area of the South China Sea before being rested.

Flt Lt James' crew had returned to Changi from Kai Tak on 7th December. On the 10th in Shackleton WB 836 they left Changi in the small hours and flew a fifteen-hour search sortie before landing at Labuan. Two further Shackleton crews, Flt Lt Jesse, WG 525 and Flt Lt Tucker in VP 291, also searched and landed at Labuan.

48 Squadron, equipped with Handley Page Hastings transport aircraft, supplied six aircraft and twelve crews for the search. On the 10th Flt Lt J.

McPhee, WD 498, Flt Lt Beard, TG580, and Flt Lt Crampton, TG 525, flew search sorties. Six Valettas and two RNZAF Freighter aircraft also flew search sorties. Two USAF Grumman Albatross aircraft were asked to search the Palewan coast.

There was an influx of ground crew to service the additional aircraft and Far East Regional Bandsmen were carried in the transport aircraft as additional eyes. I was kept busy in the bar midday and refuelling when aircraft returned as darkness fell. I then opened the bar and was extremely busy. Aircrew and the band were accommodated at the Airport Hotel with the overflow lodging with various 'Wheels'. By the time I showered and crawled into my bed I had to step over sleeping bodies on the floor on each side of my bed – at least I had a good bed and mossie net. A friend, Mick Armstrong of 205 Squadron, was like many others sleeping on racks in the stores.

Everyone worked hard and survived on very little sleep; it was known that Mike Fleetwood the OC hardly had any sleep for the duration of the search.

Thursday 11th

Flt Lt James' Shackleton crew WB 836 flew search sorties from Labuan of over eleven hours, as did Flt Lt Jesse in WG525. Hastings TG 580 Flt Lt Beard, TG 525 flown by Flt Lt Crampton and TG 531 Flt Lt W E Thomas also searched.

Search aircraft. (Photo: Author)

Search aircraft. (Photo: Author)

Search aircraft. (Photo: Author)

Search aircraft. (Photo: Author)

The hydrant refuelling system on the airfield, normally adequate for the occasional DC6 and various tiny aircraft, could not keep up the demand of the searching aircraft. As a result I had a signal from FEAF Headquarters to upgrade one of the 2500-gallon tankers to supply AVGAS. The signal detailed chapter and verse of the Fuels and Lubricants Manual, a copy of which I held, and my North Weald experience helped.

To downgrade petrol tankers to turbine fuel is simple because the turbine engine will easily accommodate a drop of AVGAS, but the piston aero engine will not tolerate the slightest whiff of kerosene. It was heavy work and involved lifting out the two large streamline filters and changing the several dozen wands, each comprising several hundred fine papers. Luckily I had them in store, refitting the filters and draining out every possible trace of kerosene. It was then necessary to load a few hundred gallons of AVGAS into the tank and pump this around the system to dilute any remaining traces of kerosene; this contaminated fuel was then to be discharged into drums and the new product could be safely loaded and used. Mr De Souza at the Shell depot was ready by mid afternoon, but I was required to operate the other tanker.

I now learned that I should always be precise in instructions and totally avoid any confusion. I knew that the two SACs could handle the lorry, and after explaining the procedure needed at the depot I told them to make sure that the first part load was 'taken', i.e. pumped around the system a few times, before discharging and reloading. They were away much longer than they should have been and aircraft were beginning to return.

I discovered that they had not been pumping the fuel around, but had thought that by 'around the system' I had meant driving around the island's road system rather than circulating the fuel in the system! Luckily the AVGAS loading system was much quicker than drums; I soon caught up with the evening's refuelling and the bar was not too late in opening.

There was not much said about any chance of survivors but it was taken as read fairly early on that there was little hope. It might sound callous but beer still flowed; I suppose it was in the tradition of 'here's to the next man to die'. Ginger, whose radio shack was extremely busy, kept me up to date with info as everything was in plain language. One Sunderland ML 797 was deployed, alighting at Labuan on the 11th, taking part in the search and returning to Seletar on 16th December.

Rod Rumsby, an airframe fitter (rigger) recalls:

My first trip to Labuan was as part of a Valetta servicing team to cope with the vast amount of A/C traffic at Labuan due to the unfortunate disappearance of one of 205's Shackletons. Virtually everything that could fly did fly and as the Shackleton had taken off from Labuan the search was concentrated around that area.

There was no room at Labuan after our transit / search flight from Changi, so we had to lob into Brunei for the first night, where we and a Hastings crew drank the bar dry by 21.00.

The next week on Labuan was hectic and we serviced not only Valettas but also Hastings Dakotas Shackletons Canberras and whatever. We were billeted in the airport hotel so didn't get to see much of the main campsite, only on the horizon so to speak. But I could see that during normal times this looked like a cushy sort of posting. Towards the end of a week or more of searching the task was scaled down and upon the discovery of the body of an aircrew member buried on a small sand spit, all aircraft bar one returned from whence they came.

The *Straits Times* reported on the Wednesday that 'the aircraft had been diverted to search for survivors of the adventure schooner *Ian Crouch* which had been missing for ten weeks' and that 'a US Navy aircraft reported seeing ten men on an island north of Labuan'. It further reported that the Shackleton had reported that a fishing boat was heading to the atoll.

Friday 12th

Flt Lt James' crew WB 836 flew search sorties from Labuan of over eleven hours, as did F/O Appleford WB 827. Flt Lt Elias flew WG 525 on this date. VP 291 returned to Labuan with the squadron commander Wg Cdr MacReady. Hastings' sorties were flown by Flt Lt J. McPhee, WD 498, Flt Lt G.E. Wright, TG 525, and Flt Lt Beard, TG 580. Coastal land searches were carried out by RAF Valettas of 52 squadron and 41 squadron RNZAF Freighter aircraft.

Another cutting on the Friday reported that an unidentified fishing vessel, which rescued 13 men, was believed to have headed for Formosa. A British registered ship the 3180 ton *Kimanis* sailed to the search area to join the 6189 ton *La Sierra* despite warnings of 'bad waters' for shipping.

Saturday 13th

On the fourth day of the search Flt /Lt James' crew WB 836 flew search sorties from Labuan of over eleven hours, as did Fg Off Appleford in Shackleton WB 827 and Flt Lt Tucker and crew in VP 291. Hastings of 48 Squadron were flown by Flt Lt G.E. Wright, TG 525, Flt Lt Beard, TG 580 and Flt Lt W.E. Thomas in TG 521.

Sunday 14th

Flt Lt Tucker in VP 291, F/Lt James, WB 836 and Fg Off Appleford, WB 827 flew search sorties from Labuan of over eleven hours. 48 Squadron provided Hastings WD 498, Flt Lt J. McPhee, TG 525, Flt Lt G.E. Wright and TG 531, Flt Lt W.E. Thomas, the last of the Hastings search sorties. Flt Lt Reynolds arrived in Hastings TG 520.

Monday 15th

On the sixth day another aircraft WG 525 flown by Flt Lt Elias started the search again at the last known position. There, on the small Sin Cowe Atoll, they spotted what appeared to be writing on the sand. On closer inspection they saw, written in coral, the sign 'B 205'. It was the missing aircraft's identification. Also on this minuscule islet they saw what appeared to be a stone cairn on which was a cross. Also searching that day was Flt Lt Tucker in WB 836.

Sin Cowe Cairn. (Photo: G. Gatcum)

B 205. (Photo: G. Gatcum)

HMNZS *Rotoiti.* (Photo: G. Gatcum)

HMS *Albion*, an aircraft carrier, was en route to Hong Kong with HMS *Chichester* and the NZ frigate *Rotoiti*. The ships were ordered to proceed to Sin Cowe to investigate. On this night I had finished refuelling quite late and had left the tanker empty. I had a shower sometime after midnight, when I was told that one of the Shackletons wanted maximum fuel load as they were to search nearer Hong Kong and land there after their search, so off I went again. I was not in bed long that night and received a bit of sympathy from some luckier souls.

151

Tuesday 16th

Before dawn two Skyraiders of 849 'C' Flight were flown off *Albion* to do a first light reconnaissance of the area. These aircraft confirmed the initial Shackleton report and brought photos of the island. In addition to Sin Cowe, the Skyraiders searched the neighbouring reefs and established that the island of Itu Aba, about thirty miles north of Sin Cowe, was the nearest inhabited island. There was no sign of life on Sin Cowe itself. The intention now was to land a search party ashore on Sin Cowe and carry out a thorough search of the island to ascertain the contents of the grave and find any message that might indicate where the possible survivors had moved.

At first it was thought that *Albion* would be able to get near enough to Sin Cowe before sunset to allow helicopters of 820 Squadron to land this search party, but in the event heavy weather slowed the ship down and the first to arrive on the scene was the *Rotoiti*, which put a whaler ashore during the afternoon.

Ken Appleford once again flew over the spot, this time directing HMNZS *Rotoiti* to the scene; he circled while they searched the cairn. The shore party carried out a preliminary search of the island before opening up the grave. They found one body in a rough coffin made of driftwood, an RAF officer's cap and a watch. Other features of the grave included a large wooden cross with the letters B 205 and an RAF roundel painted on one side, with 9 December 1958 on the reverse. Also, at one end of the line of stones covering the grave, two rice bowls had been placed. This is peculiar to the Chinese burial ritual.

Flt Lt Elias in WG 525 left Labuan on his patrol and landed in Hong Kong.

Wednesday 17th

On Wednesday 17th December *Albion* was within ten miles of Sin Cowe. The ship's log (ADM 53/148278) records that the ship spoke to HMNZS *Rotoiti* at 04.25 and two hours later the corpse was transferred by Whirlwind helicopter of 820 Squadron aboard *Albion*.

At 06.25 two helicopters with a search party were flown off to make a more detailed search of Sin Cowe island. This party included Flt Lt Hall RAF, who happened to be taking passage in *Albion* to his base at Kai Tak. It was obvious that the only regular inhabitants of the island were land crabs and turtles. On occasion fishermen had used the island, and the US Navy had made a social call, evident from a large number of beer cans around the site of a campfire.

It was decided to send the two RN officers, Lts R.H. Scott and H. Rowtowsky by helicopter to Itu Aba, where they eventually made contact with a native [sic] who could understand and write English sufficiently to answer questions, and after a while they found a fisherman who appeared to supply the answer to the mystery.

This fisherman stated he had seen the Shackleton crash into the sea from where he was fishing near Sin Cowe. He had immediately gone to the scene of the crash, although the aircraft had disappeared. He claimed that he found one airman who, although badly injured, was alive in the sea. Unfortunately this man died soon after being picked up and so the fisherman took the body to Sin Cowe and buried it there. This fisherman also went to the trouble of marking the cross and making the B 205 sign to attract the attention of the searchers.

At 14.43 two Skyraider aircraft left for Labuan with the body and grave marking cross to confirm identification and carry out a post mortem.

Ginger Jones warned the author that something was afoot as all incoming messages were now in cypher and the search was winding down. We were warned of aircraft landing mid morning and although I was busy, nobody else was around so I set off in the ambulance to stand by with the fire engines. I then spotted Ken and grabbed him for ambulance duty as he wasn't doing anything else.

Two Skyraider AEW aircraft, WT 952 (coded 422) and WT959 (coded 424) from the carrier HMS *Albion* landed and I got some photos of them

849 Sqdn Skyraiders. (Photo: Author)

153

taxiing in; unusually we were all warned to keep away from the pan. They had come ashore with the body and the other evidence that the Kiwi sailors had exhumed. There was a wooden cross, carefully jointed. On one side of the cross someone had painted the RAF tail tricolour, B 205 and a roundel; on the other side of the cross was painted 9 DEC 1958; the vertical on this side had 13 + 55 hrs TIME.

Cross from Sin Cowe reef. (Photo: Author)

Reverse side of Cross. (Photo: Author)

Cross in St Eval Church. (Photo: Author)

The body was that of the Flight Engineer F/Sgt Dancy DFC and it was taken to the local hospital in the ambulance for post mortem examination by Sqn Ldr A.B. Goorney the Changi MO assisted by Dr P.L. O'Neill, before it was taken to Changi and eventual interment at Kranji.

I had unwittingly clobbered Ken with a horrible job and he was pale and shaken for days. I felt guilty and do not know to this day if he thought I knew what was coming; I honestly had no idea.

We were all puzzled about the cross; it seemed hardly credible that a junk crew would have seen that amount of detail on a crashing aircraft, unless they were trained to report such detail or had seen it as the aircraft floated before crashing. If it did float then why were there no other bodies? Was there any evidence that the flight engineer survived long enough to identify the aircraft?

Rumour was rife and there was speculation for several years whether any crew had survived. Some members of the squadron believed that it had been shot down. The theory most discussed, and a possible cause, was that the police officer sitting lower down between the pilots was thrown or shaken in a manoeuvre and at low level knocked off the fuel cocks, leaving no time for recovery.

Flt Lt James' crew WB 836 returned to Changi on 17th December. I am obliged to M/Sig Cooper for this information from his logbook.

It was said that the crew left forty dependents, including one three-week-old baby. The cross was re-erected at St Georges Church RAF Changi where it stayed until 205 Squadron withdrew from Singapore in 1971. It is now on the wall of St Eval Church, the Coastal Command church in Cornwall, and a locally produced booklet gives details of the crash.

The total flying hours on the search were listed as 48 Squadron Hastings 180 hours. The Far East Communications Squadron Hastings flew 35. The Valettas of 52 flew 138 and the RNZAF Freighter 68 hours. The Shackletons totalled 304. The search aircraft left and we returned to normal routine.

Rod Rumsby again:

The one remaining was a Valetta that had, according to the pilot, bad brakes!!! I could find nothing wrong but he was the boss and conveyed to me his desire to get in a bit of beach time!!! So we sent to Changi for a set of brake linings and a new wheel. This gave us a day or two to take a quick look down town and sample Brodie's beach. We also discovered that Labuan was occupied by the Japs during the war and remains of various strange a/c could be found on the east side of the airfield. There was also a beautifully maintained war cemetery just down the road with lots of very young Aussies in there from when the allies took it back again.

A Singapore newspaper reported on Thursday 18th December:

It was a keen-eyed North Borneo fisherman who solved the mystery of the year here – the RAF Shackleton bomber which vanished over the China Sea on Dec 9.

An RAF spokesman told the incredible story of how the fisherman had seen the Shackleton plummet down to the sea and memorised its identification before it disappeared beneath the waves.

The fisherman had later marked the identification numbers of the crashed Shackleton in the grass on a tiny coral atoll nearby to attract searching aircraft. It was these markings that had finally led to the solution of the mystery of the missing aircraft and the end of the most intensive combined air and sea rescue operation in the history of the Far East Air Force.

The spokesman said the fisherman's story as told to a Naval landing party from HMS *Albion* yesterday proved that the 11 men aboard had died in the crash.

The newspaper reported as official the reconstruction of what happened:

The captain of a small fishing craft saw the RAF Shackleton from 205 Squadron crash into the sea near a small atoll in the Sin Cowe reef about 300 miles north of Labuan.

The fishing captain, who was a most observant man, memorised the identification number of the Shackleton before it crashed. The fishing boat went to the scene of the crash and recovered the body of one of the crew members, no other bodies or wreckage was seen.

The fisherman took the body to a nearby atoll – only two miles from their own fishing village – and buried it. They erected a makeshift cross above the grave and then cut out the markings B 205 in ten feet letters in the grass.

On 22nd December Flt Lt Elias flew Shackleton WB 836 to Labuan with memorial wreaths for the lost crew; these were dropped in the sea near Sin Cowe. Over the ensuing months there was a formal Board of Enquiry to ascertain the cause of the loss of the aircraft and crew. There were many questions: Had the aircraft stalled while turning at low level? Had there been a misjudgement of height? Were there any survivors held aboard the fishing vessel?

There was concern that a Coastal Command modification to provide a safety cover for the fuel cocks had not been completed as the aircraft had spent so long in Ministry of Aviation hands. There were several questions regarding the pilot's health and recent continuity training, and the possible height perception problems of the co-pilot who had recently converted from the Sunderland flying boat. The log of signals from the Shackleton mentioned earlier was also presented. There were comments on the suitability of using transport aircraft in the search role. It remained impossible to state accurately the cause of the crash.

Further evidence came to light about a US Navy patrol aircraft flown by Cdr Smith USN of VP-46. He had sighted the B 205 markings on Sin Cowe on 11th December but this information had not been passed on to the British. It was four days later that the markings were seen by a RAF Shackleton crew, when recovery of the body was initiated.

The fishing boat YF-890, en route to its home port Ishigaki in the Okinawan group of islands, was contacted by a US aircraft on 30th

December. YF-890 signalled it had information on survivors, but that none was aboard.

It took some time and much diplomatic activity before a statement was made available from the skipper of YF-890, made to the Chief of Yaeyama District Police Station, undated:

> Rescue of the stranded Formosan fishermen and the burial of a downed airman by *Seikai Maru* (fishing boat) and presented as Exhibit 'JA' [unclear copy J4??]

> On 9 December 1958, YF-890, 41.16 tons, a fishing boat rescued 14 stranded Formosan fishermen at Shinan-Gunto Islands (Spratly Islands) and safely delivered these men to Naga-Shima of Shinnan-Gunto where the Nationalists soldiers are stationed. An aircraft, nationality unknown, which aided this rescue operation suddenly crashed into the sea and burned with an explosion – killing all the crew. *Seikai-Maru* made a thorough search of the area recovering one body which they buried on Suna-Shima (sand bar) of Shinnan-Gunto, and returned Ishigaki Port on 10 January.

The following is the detailed information concerning the rescue and the markings on the aircraft:

> On 3 October, Captain Naka Seichi and a crew of 31, aboard fishing boat *Seikei-Maru*, left Ishigaki Port for Shinnan-Gunto to engage in collection of sea shells – arriving the destination the same day, then moved northward engaging in the shell collection. At 0830 on 9 December, she discovered an abandoned shipwreck 1/3 above sea on Shinnan-Gunto Kinyue Reef, but she continued her work, then at that time an aircraft B 205 with a crew of 4, nationality unknown, with the markings (see attached sheet* by the author [not copied]) came by, made a low altitude flight around *Seikai-Maru* and flew away. At approximately 0900 hours the aircraft came again, made a low altitude flight tipping wings, fired a single random shot as it flew away in a northeasterly direction. Fifteen minutes later the aircraft came by for the third time, made the same maneuver as before and pointed in a northeasterly direction in hand signal as it flew away. Realising this to be a distress signal, we proceeded northeasterly for 10 miles and at 1105 hours we discovered a sand bar inside Kinyue Reef. We made our approach to this and to the bar over which the B-205 was flying

around. On the sand bar people appeared to be stranded and were signaling us with a V-Flag; then the people got on two small boats (one of which was equipped with a small engine, but had no fuel) and came aboard our ship. We found them to be 14 shipwrecked Formosan fishermen who had been on the sand bar for 19 days awaiting their rescue. While this rescue was being effected the B 205 was observing our operation and as soon as rescue completed, it flew in southwesterly direction. No sooner had the aircraft flown away than two U.S. aircraft came by, flew around overhead and left us at 1350 hours.

At 1355 hours the same aircraft B 205 which was watching the rescue and flew away in southwesterly direction, flew in from the same direction at an altitude of approximately 100 meters and instantly crashed into the sea approximately 42 meters deep at 9deg 52' meridian and 114deg 19,9'.

It exploded several times as it burned and the whole area was one big ball of fire, so it was impossible to effect the rescue of the crew.

By 1430 hours, when the fire subsided, we all searched the area, and by 1510 hours we recovered one badly burned body. The search was continued until 1600 hours but no other body was discovered except one headgear. On 10 December, all of us landed on the sand bar and buried the body in the center of the sand bar where we erected a cross made out of mahogany wood on which B-205 was inscribed (by us).

After the burial, *Seikai-Maru* left this sand bar with 14 shipwrecked victims and resumed collecting operations, but on 12 December, Formosan captain requested *Seikai-Maru* their continued stay aboard was a burden upon *Seikai-Maru*, therefore they be landed near Naga-Shima (Itu Aba) where the nationalist soldiers are stationed when the right weather comes along. To comply with this request *Seikai-Maru* traveled 31 miles north of the sand bar to a point 3 miles from Naga-Shima where the shipwreck crew boarded the boat, the engine of which had been repaired and enough fuel was given them to make it to Naga-Shima. After observing the crew safely landed on the island we resumed our collecting operations.

According to Captain Naka Seichei, the downed flyer was a Caucasian and he believed the aircraft to be French. He further stated that if a photograph was taken of the down flyer he could easily have been identified. Since the crash happened so suddenly, he has no idea what caused the crash.

The name of the wrecked ship is *Zuifukusei-go*, Takae registry, 41.39 tons and it was washed against the reef in a storm. The crew landed on the sand bar nearby through the use of the life boat (engine equipped) to wait for their rescue. According to the Formosans, the U.S. aircraft came by and made food drops every two or three days, so they never experienced a food shortage.

Great doubt must be cast on the accuracy of this statement. What led him to believe there was a crew of four? Individuals sighted during the fly past, or were three bodies seen but not recovered?

No medical evidence has appeared to show the body to have been burned, neither does it seem possible as stated by the fisherman interviewed on Ibu Ata that the flight engineer could still have been alive when found by that fisherman.

It is probable that the fisherman interviewed by the two RN officers on 17th December was one of the Formosans rescued by YF-890 and put ashore on the 12th or 13th.

The sheet mentioned above marked * illustrated the details painted on the cross at the burial site of the body and appears to be accurate.

The actual cause of the crash would never be known. Audrey Hext, the sister of one of the air signallers, Sgt P.C. Barnley, carried out her own research, particularly into the inquest on the flight engineer F/Sgt Dancy. She travelled to Borneo some years later and carried out several interviews and remains convinced that the statement given by Captain Naka Seichi was inaccurate and completed purely for financial reasons.

It is difficult to know whether the American aircraft in the area were already involved in the search for the vessel *Ian Crouch* when the Shackleton was diverted, which might account for the signal 'USAF B 29 arrived'. They might well have been involved in reconnaissance during the tense period of the disputed Quemoy Islands / Taiwan Strait bombardment battles between the Communist and Nationalist armies.

Cdr Smith USN flying an aircraft of VP-46 sighted the cairn 'B 205' on Sin Cowe on 11th December, but this information was not passed to the British and only revealed later at the Board of Enquiry. This was four days before the RAF spotted it and set about the recovery of the body. It also illustrated that the Americans had their own agenda and were unlikely to cooperate, unless it was in their own interest. The actual fate of the adventure schooner *Ian Crouch*, the original reason for the diversion from the anti-piracy patrol, is uncertain, but it is understood to have got to Hong Kong safely.

Leaving Labuan, 1959

Before Christmas 1958 the American Embassy people came through for another shopping trip. I was greeted by one who said, 'Hey, Dave, I thought you would be Mayor of this place by now.' At Christmas, my fourth abroad since joining the RAF, we had a competition for which billet had the best bar; ours was a gaudy affair with old supply parachutes as the main decoration.

We took some time off and Mike Fleetwood played a blinder in serving Christmas dinner; he also iced a cake, something he had learned from his father. Much drink was consumed and on Boxing Day we had an excellent cold buffet.

Early in 1959 we had another naval visit, this time from the Indian Navy ships, INS *Thir* and INS *Caudery*; they were small ships and had originally been RN vessels. A full programme of sports was held between them and civilian and service teams but there was no rugby. We had them on the unit for a drink or two and I talked to a Sikh chief petty officer over a few beers. He told me that he regretted the absence of National Service as he thought it would help unite India as a nation.

I was at a loose end one Sunday morning and persuaded the Borneo Airways engineer that I should have a ride when he did an air test in one of the Twin Pioneers. The take-off took only a matter of yards, the ascent was like a lift. We left the ground near the DF hut and it appeared to get smaller and smaller with little sensation of forward movement.

The array of slats and flaps was impressive. He then threw it around at low level near a small island lighthouse and I was airsick but did not spill a drop. The approach to land was slow and amusing: as we drifted in over the road I saw a young lad stop and dismount from his bike, look up and wave, all of this as we passed him. The ground crew were amused at me clutching my sick bag, despite which I thoroughly enjoyed the flight.

We had a visit from Air Marshal the Earl of Bandon CB DSO, the AOCinC, who came in his VIP Valetta and brought his wife. He was a very popular man and beloved by most airmen because of his reputation. He had formally opened the new swimming pool at Changi and then dived in, fully dressed in uniform.

There was no formal parade or schedule but I made sure that the MT was OK and tidied every bit of rubbish from my office table. The great man and Mike the OC called on me last of all, and Paddy, the Earl, decided that he needed to list all that had been discussed through the day. He took my seat and asked for some paper, which I had difficulty in finding. He was very affable and sat there and asked Mike to remind him, '... more lockers ... I think he should be a Corporal ... hmm what were the other things?' I found myself humming and hawing with them. Less than a week later a Freighter flew in with extra lockers and one of the lads put up his corporal's stripes earlier than he had expected.

February 1959 saw the second leg of Sabre Ferry with a total of sixteen Sabres of No 77 Squadron RAAF flying through; we refuelled them and sent them on their way. 77 Squadron had fought with Meteors in Korea. I had not realised until reading their squadron history *Swift To Destroy* that they had been part of the Australian force that took Labuan back from the Japanese in 1945.

One major difference in the second ferry was that they were supported by the first of the RAAF Hercules. It had taken seven Dakotas to move No 3 Squadron, whereas it only took two Hercules for this move. When this big shiny beast landed, the crew were greeted by some other Aussies who made comments about the comparison. 'Beats the goony bird any day,' was the reply.

I needed both refuellers but had to connect the DP to the Hercules and simultaneously fill that from the old open line tanker, having no idea at that

RAAF C 130 Hercules. (Photo: Author)

77 Sqdn RAAF CAC Sabre A 94 977. (Photo: Author)

77 Sqdn RAAF CAC Sabre A 94 967. (Photo: Author)

time how hazardous free-falling fuel could be. The Aussie engineer had to show all concerned how he could simply switch the fuel from the fuelling point, and worried me by filling the other side first and putting the aircraft at quite an angle, but he had to show off his new toy. The RAF was not to get the Hercules until seven years later.

Came Chinese New Year and we had a fine time: the club was given over to gambling, almost a religion to the Chinese. The town was ankle deep in paper from firecrackers and we were invited to drinks and snacks by the owner of the Cold Store bar.

Prince Philip was on a world tour mainly using the Royal Yacht but flying between some places. We were told that we were to line the path into the new airport terminal building at Jesselton (Kota Kinabulu) on the mainland. He flew from Singapore to Kuching in a Heron of the Royal Flight followed by a para-equipped Valletta, carrying the Jungle Rescue team from Changi, with a Shackleton covering low level and the CinC's Valetta as standby for the Heron. He then went on in the Royal Yacht *Britannia* and the Valetta and Heron landed at Labuan. Mere mortals were not allowed near the Heron; it was polished in the early hours by the crew, including the wing commander captain.

The Queen's Flight D H Heron XH 375. (Photo: Author)

On the Sunday we flew across to the mainland in the Valetta at low level sitting in the para nets and with no doors on; it was cool and very pleasant. Our host was the Chief Officer of Borneo Railways. He told us that various tribes had been brought down and given materials to build their exhibits and a rum ration to last the duration of the royal visit. This rum they had drunk on the first night and without a daily ration would do no more. One of the 'Wheels' with the only open car on the mainland had it bought and repainted for 'himself' to drive by.

We changed into our gear and lined up, to hear the tetchy comment, 'What are these people doing here?' I noticed the Marine Superintendent opposite taking a photo of the great man with his lens covered. Following the formalities we toured the displays: one was a platform within a hut where the tribe danced and sang as the sprung wooden floor bounced. In another was a flask of rice wine where a straw was offered to lower the level of the drink. Ken Lupton, the chef, did his turn and was almost instantly drunk. We had a good day and flew back to Labuan the same evening.

During one of the busy spells I had to refill one of the trucks again. Tiger and his young Jock assistant came to the fuel depot to help. As I turned into the fuel depot road I was glad I was not alone, for I saw the weirdest dog-sized prehistoric-looking animal in the road. The other two confirmed they had seen it; it was an iguana, not a delusion.

The OC persuaded me that we could afford to use the Bedford truck to carry a World Health Organization team to various places around the island where they were spraying DDT as an anti-malarial campaign. Much criticised later by environmentalists, it was an essential matter for health at that time.

My replacement Gerry was in place. He was a keen runner; I used to help him with his training by riding alongside on my bike. It did not take long to hand over the section and I plotted to get the best trip back that I could. I tried to go via Kuching with the two Czechoslovakians flying the 81 Squadron Pembroke, but was told that there were not enough beds available in the hotel.

81 Squadron Pembroke. (Photo: Author)

On 2nd March 1959 I left Labuan. The CinC's Valetta was flying back empty, and together with Pete (Eccles) Faulkner and the rest of the Seletar fitting party I travelled back to Changi in sheer luxury. A memorable detachment on an interesting island. Back to the bustling RAF Seletar and, after a brief local leave, to a new job.

More Labuan Stories

Rod Rumsby supplied more memories of his time in Labuan:

I cannot agree with the statement that there was not a lot to do in Labuan, I had two spells there in the fifties and found myself fully occupied. Very little of which was on behalf of Her Majesty, work coming low on the priorities list. The beaches were remarkable and deserted, the sea was clear and full of interesting creatures, can't for the life of me remember her name now. For those interested in ulu bashing, most of the island was an undiscovered delight, her name escapes me too, the local bars rarely closed and the eggs curry in *tay soo hie*'s was to die for. OK the cinema was basic but cost only 50c and was as up to date with films as Changi. I was able to import my motor cycle from Changi so was more able to find parts that other blokes couldn't, she was a cracker as well.

Yes I liked Labuan so much I extended my 6 months to finish my tour at Labuan, I just served on quietly saying nothing until they caught up with me in October 1960 and stuck me on another troopship for Blighty after three years of hell in the ulu (liar). To be honest Singers was in the throes of a make over at that time and I was not sorry to leave.

The bar was run by a Cpl but the beer supply was on draught, Tiger naturally, but there was also a good range of German type lagers. Food was excellent as the Chef was a drinking partner and could easily be persuaded to knock up something homely or even exotic if plied with enough booze.

One of the Borneo Airways Twin Pioneers, on landing on a little airstrip somewhere in the state of Brunei managed to clip a tree that inexplicably leapt out in front of it, don't they always. It was beyond repair on site so it was dismantled (by Borneo Airways staff) and floated downriver and across the short stretch of oggin on a barge, landing at port Victoria in Lab. The intention being then to tow the wingless fuselage up the road to the airport. The only 4 × 4 on the island at that time capable of pulling the thing up the hill was thought to be an RAF Land Rover (MkI version). However it proved to have clutch problems and couldn't make the long pull without a strong smell of smouldering asbestos permeating the environment.

The Twin Pin sat on the quay for a time, while the search went on for a good towing vehicle. This arrived in the form of a brand new Toyota Land Cruiser, just imported in from Japan. The scoffing continued late into the night, anything Japanese in those days was considered to be not only vastly inferior but rather suspect considering their pretty recent hostilities on the island. The next morning the much maligned Toyota sailed up the hill trailing one Twin Pin, which was going almost as fast backwards as it usually did in forward flight.

The very proud owner of this quite massive (compared to our little Land Rover) product of Japan was only too pleased to allow us chagrined Brits to check out his new toy (no pun intended). It looked much like a jeep from the front, no surprise there, but much bigger and it had a beautiful six-cylinder OHV engine under the bonnet. So my introduction to the new age of Japanese mastery of the roads began that day, made worse by the admission of the driver that he had had no need to select four wheel drive or even low ratio for the tow.

I have been trying to recollect some of the more dramatic happenings during my stay there, but nothing springs to mind, I just had a real good time. We were interrupted by the odd aircraft arrival whilst searching for local colour, bundu bashing, taking my motor bike along impossible jungle trails, or better still hareing (sic) along at a rate of knots on the wide sandy beaches to the north east of the island. We discovered the remains of an old coalmine at the northern tip of the island (you could just see the chimney from the airport by standing on top of a Beverley).

We played rugby against a crew from a visiting Australian destroyer; I think we barely lost that one. We took a frightening trip across the 'oggin in a couple of dugout canoes, towed by the PSI boat to a little island Papan? with a lighthouse on it.

After an AOC's, he reported that our flight line stores (a tin hut if I recall) was not big enough to house the large items of ground equipment needed to support the Beverleys. So we were sent a quite large canvas hangar (Spitfire size) with a flat pack steel frame. We of the aircraft trades successfully erected this on a piece of ground just outside the billet wherein we kipped. A magnificent achievement, well we thought so.

On one of our bundu bashing treks we stumbled across the remains of an old pineapple plantation. We had been slashing our way through the brush for hours and were dehydrated, hungry and knackered, so when we found a few smallish pineapples still growing we put our parangs to good use. Now I hate pineapple, but that day it was nectar.

At one time the runway was restricted by a repair gang and the only visiting i.e. mail a/c allowed were Dakotas of 1325 Flight, formerly used on Christmas Island and then based at Changi, so we had a pretty unproductive period, more bundu bashing.

The closure of the airfield led to questions in the House of Commons about the proposed length of closure for resurfacing and extent of navigational aids and night flying facilities available, bearing in mind the strategic position of the airfield. The Colonial Secretary assured the MP that navigational aids and flarepath would be provided by the Royal Air Force.

Sandy Boyd, a telegraphist, while at RAF Changi, mentioned to his supervisor that when working Labuan the operator was always too fast for him. The supervisor rectified matters by sending Sandy to Labuan as a replacement where he worked for Cpl McMurdo.

The late Eric Pursglove wrote in *The Haltonian*; the date is unknown:

'The OC Labuan held regular project meetings when possible visits or items of interest were discussed. One such item was the Labuan Gun. There had been a long standing friendly dispute between the Detachment and the Labuan Resident as to who would recover it and outside whose HQ it would eventually stand. Eric was requested to consider the feasibility of recovering the gun and its mounting.

The gun was a 120mm Japanese naval piece originally sited to defend the site against attack from the south west. It lay in a deep thickly overgrown dugout in a known snake infested area. With a 100 per cent turn out of volunteers the gun was taken to the detachment.'

Like the author, John Lambert, a corporal air radio fitter, found himself in March 1961 to be the only unaccompanied man at RAF Changi in his trade and duly flew to Labuan in a Bristol Freighter of 41 Squadron RNZAF. On arrival he had a very quick briefing from the man he was relieving. He joined the other aircraft tradesmen, one of each trade, who had for many years serviced the passing transient aircraft of all types.

Transient traffic proved to be very light for some time as the old coral pan was removed and replaced – the regular Bristol Freighter of 41 Squadron, an occasional Twin Pioneer or Canberra on photo-reconnaissance and a

Beverley with Ghurkha troops aboard. A Valetta with ignition loom problems caused the turbine-trained engine man a major headache.

The canvas hangar, generally known as the Spitfire hangar, was also removed. It was amusing locally to see the snow limitation markings, 'Unsafe in more than five inches of snow'. The original Bessoneau hangar had snow beams and specific instructions that they be lowered between November and April; hardly necessary at Labuan.

The sole soldier (Troops) job was to repair the lines from the W/T hut to the transmitters. If anything went wrong he didn't bother to find the fault, as the plans were so out of date. He just laid a new line!

The OC Detachment at that time was Flt Lt M.J.W. Pierson, a navigator, who John was to meet in later years. John remustered to aircrew and in 1972 joined 206 Squadron at RAF Kinloss, finding that Wg Cdr Pierson was the OC 206.

Brunei Rebellion, 1962

Between 1959 and 1962 Britain, Malaya, Singapore, Sarawak and British North Borneo were involved in negotiations to form a new Malaysian Federation. The Philippines and Indonesia opposed any move towards unification of Sarawak within the new Federation. There were many elements in the territories of North Borneo, Brunei and Sarawak who would have preferred to have a North Borneo Federation.

Political forces within Sarawak had anticipated their own national independence as promised by the last White Rajah in 1941. Groups among Sarawak's urban Chinese supported the unification of British Borneo territories, which was seen as a post-colonial alternative to the Malaysian Federation. Local opposition throughout the Borneo territories was based on economic, political and cultural differences between the Borneo states and the Malayan peninsula and reluctance to be subjected to peninsular political domination.

There had been rumours of the existence of a Borneo Liberation Army as early as June of that year and in November the authorities in Kuching were warned by the British Resident in the Fifth Division that 'political intrigue seemed to be going on'. On 7th December the Commissioner General for South East Asia, at the conclusion of a routine visit to Brunei, informed the Commander-in-Chief in Singapore that a rebel attack on either the Sarawak oilfield at Miri or on that belonging to Brunei at Seria was a distinct possibility. HQ Far East Air Force (FEAF) had an up to date plan ALE to reinforce the Brunei Police, and the appropriate force was brought to immediate readiness. In December 1962 the RAF Detachment Labuan, normally with a Flight Lieutenant in charge, remained as a Detachment but with Wing Commander J.R.C.H. Graves commanding. Additional technical tradesmen included fifty-two from Changi and fourteen from the UK, as well as four telegraphists direct from the UK. When rebellion broke out as forecast on 8th December the British forces were fully prepared and went into action immediately.

HMS *Albion*, commissioned as a commando carrier on exercise off the East African coast, received a signal on 9th December to proceed with all despatch to Singapore in order to pick up reinforcements for Borneo.

Twelve Hastings of 48 Squadron, four Beverleys of 34 Squadron and Twin Pioneers of 209 Squadron started the airlift of two companies of Ghurkha Rifles to Brunei. The pilot of the first Beverley, Sqn Ldr M.G. Bennett DFC reconnoitred the airfield, reported by Labuan control to be blocked, but on inspection he found that obstacles had been removed. He successfully landed ninety-three troops and the Ghurkhas took over the airfield.

209 Squadron had been alerted at RAF Seletar on Sunday 9th December 1962 that three Twin Pioneer aircraft, with immediate servicing back up, were to move to Labuan on the following day. This aircraft, known by many in the RAF as the Twin Pin, was only referred to on 209 as the Twin or T.E.P (Twin engine Pioneer). Vic Dabin, a pilot on 209, had recently been liaising with the Police Field Force in Kuching with no mention or knowledge of forthcoming political problems.

The squadron already had two aircraft engaged on anti-piracy at Tawau. The three aircraft, carrying spare crews, flew in extremely unpleasant weather, a mixture of thunderstorms, low cloud, heavy rain and strong winds, on the first leg of 400 miles to Kuching. The ground crews turned the aircraft round ready for the final leg in monsoon weather. The Chinese controller told them of terrible overnight events in Brunei.

The weather reports from Labuan and nearby airstrips were very poor, the CO advising that in normal circumstances he would not ask them to continue but these were not normal circumstances. They flew to Labuan in a loose gaggle in strong winds and torrential rain, keeping the coast in sight, reaching Labuan after a total of eight hours' flying and in hope of a quiet beer.

Vic was advised that he was to fly to Brunei with blood for those injured in the fighting. By now it was dark and the weather was even worse. Brunei airfield, scarcely visible in the gloom, was not yet secure and the soldiers did not want any aircraft to remain, so an immediate return was made to Labuan. The return was made at wave-top level and the landing nearly catastrophic as an unknown Land Rover crossed their path as he was about to land.

With no other available people the aircrew were then engaged in marshalling the larger transport aircraft to enable them to disgorge the reinforcements without stopping their engines. At 04.30 they were relieved by airmen from Changi who took over the marshalling and servicing duties.

A Britannia of Transport Command at Changi was commandeered; the aircraft was turned around in just over the hour by the Labuan staging post airmen and was able to complete two round trips from Changi in the day.

On 8th and 9th December twenty-eight transport aircraft loads were flown into Brunei, including reinforcement for the staging post on Labuan. Air Chief Marshal Sir David Lee states, 'The small staging post party on the airfield at Labuan worked around the clock with remarkable energy and efficiency in deplaning troops, vehicles and equipment and turning the aircraft around.'

After a brief sleep in an overcrowded Airport Hotel and a hurried breakfast, Vic Dabin reported to the makeshift operations room. He was tasked with picking up a small party of army and police at Brunei to take them to the coast immediately to the west of Brunei to confirm that an earlier reconnaissance made by Norman Lamb was suitable. Vic was able to assure the planners that a strip of land around 400 yards long should be acceptable. It was near the Shell management married quarters, west of the Seria oilfield, near a place called Panaga.

Back at Labuan on 10th December the crews were briefed on the proposed operation to secure the release of hostages held by the rebels in Panaga Police Station. Five Twin Pioneers would insert troops of 1st Battalion of The Queens Own Highlanders (QOH) into the strip at Panaga, while simultaneously a Beverley with troops would land on the grass airfield at Anduki to the east of Seria, thus forming a pincer operation.

The troops would be picked up at Brunei; to enable rapid deplanement the aircraft doors were removed and the troops given practice before embarking on the flight. Vic was due to fly as the third aircraft in the stream. The second detailed aircraft had difficulty in starting, so the remainder took off and flew out to sea at low level to await the second aircraft. A QOH officer then told Vic it was essential to ensure the planned order of landing was maintained and that he must follow the second aircraft. Because the rebels might have been listening, the use of R/T was forbidden. Vic and his navigator decided to use cricketing terms over the R/T and tell the others that the captain insisted that the planned batting order must be maintained, or they would be out for a 'duck'. The other pilots quickly understood and the second aircraft rejoined in its correct position.

Meanwhile a Beverley of 34 Squadron with 110 troops aboard landed at Anduki, deplaning and taking off 1 minute and 48 seconds later. These troops split up and soon captured the airfield and its buildings.

As the Beverley would already have landed and the element of surprise was lost, the Twin Pioneer crews began to use R/T in plain language. The leader ordered the others to orbit while he set up a left-hand circuit to land from the south. Vic followed the second aircraft, having been ordered to land as close as possible, but to leave enough space for the preceding aircraft to take off. The leader floated some way before touch down. Vic noticed much mud and water and watched the first to land just stop before the monsoon drain at the end of the strip. The troops quickly disembarked and the leading aircraft cleared before the second landed. The leader advised landing from the north, but by this time the second had landed without further incident but confirmed the wet and slippery conditions.

Vic turned and made his landing from the north, advising the troops that features would be on the opposite side to their briefing. He set up a very short landing in order to take off using the remainder of the strip. Vic described his three-point landing as more like a controlled crash, as he juggled the throttles and turned to miss a bush and stopped within 150 yards. There was plenty of space to take off, but Vic saw that he had sunk up to the main wheel axles in mud. He did not want to be bogged down and obstruct further landings so he selected full power and despite another soft patch slowing the run, he 'hauled her off into a shuddering climb and the Twin, with her flying properties of a man lifting kite, staggered over the jungle tops just above the stall'.

The navigator later remarked that the load of troops had been covered in mud and dirty water as they left due to Vic's application of full power. Some years later Vic, an accomplished artist, presented a painting of his aircraft 970 to one of the Highlanders who had arrived in the second aircraft. After taking more troops from Brunei to the grass airfield at Lutong Miri they returned to Labuan.

The air landing operation had been successful, with no loss of British lives; the hostages had been released and the troops had relieved the Panaga Police Station. It was considered to have been the first air-landed assault, other than glider borne, since Iraq in the mid-1930s.

Jeff Jefford in *The Flying Camels* records that a 45 Squadron Canberra flew Major Waterton and Mr Pumphrey to Labuan on the 8th; another 45 crew flew Brigadier Glennie, who was to set up Joint Force Headquarters, and Capt Whitehead on the following day.

Sir David Lee continues, '... on the following day the weather deteriorated but both Pioneers and Beverleys flew reinforcements into Anduki in torrential rain, an operation which reflected great credit on the aircrew.'

During this operation, on the 11th, Canberra WH 969 of 45 Squadron detached at Labuan flew a number of dummy attacks low over the rebels, who then agreed not to harm their hostages. The squadron history states, 'the rebels had been talking to the Shell representative at Seria by telephone threatening the hostages, already taken as a shield, in an attack on the police post. As the Canberra roared over, a new voice came on the line and promised that no harm would befall the hostages.'

A similar ploy was used by four 20 Squadron Hunters when they staged a mock attack on Seria Police Station, one aircraft firing its guns over the building and into the sea. This was followed by a broadcast from a 209 Squadron 'Voice' Pioneer calling on the rebels to surrender. Immediately after the broadcast a British platoon stormed the police station and rescued forty-eight European hostages.

During the next eleven days the airlift continued unabated, every aircraft being pressed into service. These included an RNZAF Bristol Freighter of 41 Squadron, an RAAF Hercules, Shackletons of 205 Squadron, a Valetta of 52 Squadron and a Britannia alternately operated by crews of 99 and 511 Squadrons.

HMS *Albion* arrived in Singapore on 13th December and left soon after for Borneo.

By the thirteenth day after the revolt broke out, the airlift had taken into Brunei over 3000 passengers, over 100 vehicles, including a refueller, assorted guns and trailers, two Auster aircraft and over 600,000 lb of freight; the well-developed facilities at Labuan permitted such a large influx.

45 Squadron continued to fly to Labuan throughout the month of December, carrying out another shipping reconnaissance on the 12th and several passenger flights delivering senior Army Air Force and Naval officers.

The twin rotor Belvedere helicopter, developed by Bristol and produced by Westland, became known through the following campaign as the Flying Longhouse. On 18th December three Belvedere of 66 Squadron deployed the 750 miles to Labuan in an eight-hour ferry flight, a helicopter record at that time.

In view of the paucity of good airfields in the area, a great strain was placed upon RAF Labuan and it was remarkable that so large a force could be deployed with such rapidity. Thirty casualties and seven dead were evacuated to RAF Hospital Changi.

For this campaign, in suppressing the Brunei rebellion, the General Service Medal Army RAF 1918 and the Naval General Service Medal was awarded with a clasp Brunei, for action between 8th December and 23rd December 1962. This was to have been the sixteenth and final clasp for these medals; however a retrospective award was made for the Canal Zone in 2003 for service in the Suez Canal Zone between 1951 and 1954. Following this campaign the General Service Medal 1962–2007 was introduced for all three services.

Confrontation, 1963

The term *Konfrontasi* (Confrontation) was coined by President Sukarno of Indonesia following the formation of the Independent Federation of Malaysia in September 1963. British North Borneo (Sabah) and Sarawak were two of the constituent parts of the island of Borneo.

845 Squadron Fleet Air Arm, equipped with Wessex helicopters, had deployed from HMS *Albion* to Kuching, then Miri, Seria and Brunei until being detached to Labuan in early January 1963; 845 had a busy month helping in flood relief.

HMS *Albion* started trooping operations in February carrying 1st Battalion, 7th Ghurkha Rifles and 1st Kings Own Yorkshire Light Infantry to Brunei Bay. For the rest of the year *Albion* spent most of her time transporting various air squadrons and troops to, from, and around North Borneo. On her fifth run she carried 42 Commando and the 1st Battalion, The Royal Green Jackets, back from Labuan to Singapore. The ship operated light fixed wing aircraft (Army Austers, Beavers and RAF Single Pioneers) from her deck – an operation watched at first with interest and caution, as the ship had no arrester wires or barrier. During December 1963 two Twin Pioneers of Royal Malaysian Air Force (RMAF) arrived. HMS *Albion* disembarked the Kings Own Yorkshire Light Infantry, relieving The Green Howards who embarked on *Albion*. Two Pioneer aircraft of 209 Squadron flew off *Albion*'s flight deck; Belvedere helicopters shuttled under slung loads during the changeover.

From the start of air supply operations until 1965, 55 Air Despatch Company RASC were responsible for air despatch of air dropped cargo at Labuan. The Royal Air Force had a lot to learn in supporting the army in such an environment from what was initially a small underdeveloped base. The attitude of airmen involved varied according to their experience; many relished being involved in such an active unit in an entirely new environment. Many had moved from comfortable stations where they had enjoyed a nine to five existence. The squadron tradesmen based in Singapore on a fixed tour were used to occasional detachments but now experienced a more hectic existence. Among some airmen involved there was resentment about serving a fixed tour at Labuan alongside airmen who had the opportunity of going back to their families in Singapore.

The communications tradesmen probably had the worst deal; the individual trades were undermanned and spent very little time in the UK between tours. Almost without exception, airmen appreciated the gradual improvement in conditions, although many preferred the lack of formality of the early days before the arrival of such people as the Station Warrant Officer (SWO).

Brian Roche served in Ground Comms, arriving early in 1963; he was billeted alongside the airfield at Labuan and was later moved to Membedai. There were about thirty staff in total, providing initial air-ground communications for airfield plus longer range MF and secure HF communication to units in the field. There was a rapid build-up over the next few months. At one time the main generator caught fire and systems had to be powered by small Petbow units.

RAF Labuan. (Photo: via Brian Roche)

Brian Turner was an air wireless mechanic on 209 Squadron sent to Labuan in May 1963. Usually working in a small workshop, he did manage an air test on a single engine Pioneer, combined with mail delivery to Brunei.

Tented site. (Photo: via Brian Roche)

The routine was to spend a month at a time at base; alternate months away were spent at Kuching or Labuan.

Because of their light weight the Pioneers were picketed down; designed for short take-off, it was not unknown for a single to take off almost immediately after unpicketing, or in a strong cross wind to land across the runway. Brian does think that the pilot got a rocket for the latter event.

209 Single and Twin Pioneers. (Photo: Boyd)

Four months after detachment duties had started, Brian remarked that the improvement in accommodation was almost unbelievable. One memory was of talking to a SAS corporal awaiting return to Singapore; he told of living

179

with Dayak and of infiltration, Brian was sure he must have been ready for return to civilisation. A message arrived telling the trooper he was going back up country: 'His face lit up with joy, have one on me.' Brian thought he must be mad.

Later in the month Argosy aircraft of 215 Squadron arrived. Ten Twynham huts arrived in an effort to provide improved accommodation. During May Beverley XB264 of 34 Squadron had an engine problem; a replacement was flown in aboard XB 260. Adrian Burge has posted photos of this event on the Beverley website.

On 4th August 1963 Wg Cdr W.E. Thomas AFC assumed command vice Wg Cdr J.R.C.H. Graves. The established strength was fourteen officers and 162 airmen, the officers being accommodated at Labuan Airport Hotel.

Tony Ridley recalls:

My first trip to Labuan was shortly after the confrontation with Indonesia started. I was a Cpl. rigger on 34 Squadron and was in Calcutta in order to ship Europeans from the Assam border. We were there a week and only flew once; for some reason the Hastings did all the flying.

We left India at 2 hours notice and it took 6 weeks for the mess bills to catch us up. A long flog back to Seletar, 20 hours on the ground, just time to get the dhobi done, Tiger and legover then takeoff for Labuan. We relieved the guys who had gone with the original Beverleys and had been working solid for the past five days, we at least would only be doing 24 on 24 off.

For this trip sleeping was in what was, up until then, the cinema, 36 guys (not all of 34 Squadron) in total, hot bedding on 18 camp beds. Food, no problem, bread & margarine, sausage, egg and beans every meal, any time day or night. They do reckon that the local baker's bread tins didn't cool down for 3 months. We were told that we would be there for Christmas, so we resigned ourselves to that, and all the wives in Singapore made their own arrangements. On the 22nd December the powers that be swapped the squadron personnel over, thus screwing up everyone's Christmas, but I suppose that is typical 'cockup power'.

From then on it was month and month about, Labuan – Singapore; it was an interesting fact that the tan one got in Labuan was far superior to the Singapore one. Dress was very informal, flip-flops, shorts and a sweat rag. I remember my mate Eddie W, t'other rigger, was wiping the freight bay floor with rag and paper towels after bringing back some dead personnel from up country. Unfortunately the rough coffins had leaked not only there but onto the forklift as well; the pongo driver asked for some of the special fluid Eddie was using, so Eddy sold him a gallon for $10 to clean his forklift.

It was Eddie who had hidden behind the main spar when landing at Anduki to offload the Ghurkhas. The Beverley didn't stop; they jumped out of the para doors shortly after landing, the captain threw it round 180, gave it full boost, took off again, and got a bullet through the boom Elsan for good measure. The water tank was later mounted and placed in the squadron crew room in Singapore.

Pete Rushen recalls:

I only did three-month stints at Labuan with 34 Sqdn. when the Confrontation sh1t hit the fan. The first three months was great, lived in a tent on the edge of the pan, the office was another tent & role equipment was kept in the third. Dress was flip flops and PT shorts, when the shorts got dirty you washed them out in a bucket of green (100/130 Avgas) and whirled them around your head to let it evaporate.

Second time there it was 'organised'. A SWO had been shipped in; you had to wear regulation dress with your socks rolled up. Humbug! The town & food was always good, as was the beach. Very rarely flew in the afternoon as cloud had built up so no supply drops. Off to the beach.

John Feltham remembers:

52 Sqdn had two Valettas permanently based in Labuan together with a ground crew of one of each trade except for the airframes and engines – there were two of them. Each aircraft stayed on station for a period of around four to six weeks. As each aircraft came up for a major inspection it was replaced by another Valetta from Butterworth. The ground crew were relieved (in more ways than one) by a fresh crew from Butterworth.

I suppose that I did about 6 detachments in total. It was a miserable place to be. Just like those at Gan, we used to gather round the aircraft stairs of all Transport Command aircraft arriving from the UK. I don't recall ever seeing a woman get off an aircraft though – unlike at Gan, what was there to do in Labuan? There was a beach but I can't remember ever swimming in the sea there.

There was a nice building called 'The Shell Club', the Membedai, used by the officers. I do however recall getting in a lot of pit time; we slept in hastily built long houses, open to the elements at both ends. We were issued with the old camp bed; that had a habit of rolling over and tipping you out during the night, mosquito nets had to be used. We made a timber bed frame and hung the camp bed from the frame thus stopping the thing from rolling over.

I was present when a whole bunch of UK SAS squaddies got off a Britannia. They were all carrying short-barrelled pump action shot guns. I asked one of the squaddies if they (the guns) were banned under the Geneva Convention. 'Yes he said, but the other side hasn't signed it yet.'

Raymond Rees Oliviere recalls:

This was another spot for us 110 Squadron Crewmen, just after the Brunei stint. Our Squadron Mascot, the monkey that used to live in our billet. When at Labuan with the 'chopper', I used to take care of him. The beggar always had to chew into my toothpaste tube, drink my tea and chatter away when he saw me.

I took him to the squadron one day and the devil tore up some of the Form 700 pages. Got a 'rollicking' from the CO for that little caper. Great little guy. I only hope he was looked after when I went down to Kuching and back to Singapore.

On 30th September 845 Squadron embarked on HMS *Albion* to be replaced by 103 Squadron. At this time the first airmen arrived on a one-year posting from UK as opposed to a detachment from elsewhere in the Far East Air Force (FEAF).

Following continuing incursions by Indonesian aircraft an Air Defence Identification Zone (ADIZ) was established and on 5th October Hunters of 20 Squadron and two Javelins of 60 Squadron arrived from Tengah. Rules of Engagement allowed pilots to engage and destroy Indonesian aircraft over-flying the ADIZ, without further authority from the ground.

Bill Hyland did several detachments to Labuan flying as a navigator on Javelins with 60 Squadron and in his own words found the flying to be quite interesting.

The policy in November 1963 was to provide a base in East Malaysia to receive reinforcements as required. The airfield was to support transport aircraft in support of operations, and to provide aircraft with an alternative route to Australia and the West Pacific. To provide a base and support for Royal Malaysian Air Force (RMAF) aircraft deployed to Labuan. Aircraft based at Labuan were to be: one Beverley, one Valetta, four Twin Pioneer, two Pioneer aircraft, up to twelve Whirlwind or Belvedere helicopters. Transient Hastings or Argosy, not exceeding two at any one time.

For opposition to Indonesian aggression:

Argosy or Hastings up to 3 aircraft
Transient Britannia   1 aircraft
D F / G A Fighter up to 10 aircraft
All Weather Fighter up to 4 aircraft
Canberra   up to 6 aircraft

For SEATO: A maximum of 6 Shackleton, a temporary detachment of 4 Canberra.

Labuan was to be self-accounting, but to remain parented by Changi until reorganisation [AIR28/1693]. By this time the establishment, less detached personnel, had risen to twenty officers and 249 airmen.

Two Whirlwind helicopters flown by Fg/Off Symons of 110 Squadron and Master Pilot Stubbs of 103 were hit by automatic weapons fire. The padre Wg Cdr A.M. Ross, a passenger in an Auster of 7 Recce Flight, 665 Squadron, was wounded by ground fire and died of his injuries. During 1963 Casualty Evacuation (Casevac) aircraft returned to Singapore with nine bodies and a total of forty-two stretcher and walking wounded cases.

The radar convoy arrived from El Adem in December 1963, shortly afterwards to become No 129 Signals Unit. The first commanding officer was Sqn Ldr J.H. Lacey DFM*, one of the highest-scoring fighter pilots during the Battle of Britain, credited with 28 kills and with the distinction of being on active service at the beginning and end of the 1939–45 war. He was known worldwide as 'Ginger' Lacey, and he died aged 72 in May 1989.

The equipment, comprising nine RVT vehicles, was installed on the HF transmitter site behind the ammunition dump on the far side of the airfield and operated, initially during daylight hours only and from February 1964, on a four-watch system. During this month a Comet of 51 Squadron flew an eavesdropping Signals Intelligence (Sigint) sortie down the eastern coast of Borneo, landing in Darwin. A Pembroke WV 752 was established for communications duties.

Visiting officers were Wg Cdr Graves and Sqn Ldr Benett DFC, en route to be awarded the Most Blessed Order of Setia Negara Brunei (Class 3) by the Sultan of Brunei, for their part in the suppression of the earlier Brunei revolt.

The Labuan Catholic history notes that Fr Dassen had very good relations with the British Forces and that he was able to obtain free food for the Orphanage, not a subject normally to be admitted in a War Diary or Form 540.

On one trooping trip *Albion* gave a lift to one of *Ark Royal*'s groups. *Ark Royal* was unable to sail due to mechanical problems so 815 Squadron was transferred to *Albion* to be transported to North Borneo and deployed ashore at Labuan.

These anti-submarine warfare helicopters retained their ASW colour scheme and must have been an unusual sight in the jungle in their bright livery. On 12th August *Albion* sailed for apparently just another trooping run which became rather complicated. The sequence was Singapore – Kuching – Labuan – Kuching – Brunei Bay – West of Kuching, Singapore bound – Kuching – Singapore. During this period, apart from replenishing and exercising, the ship transported miscellaneous air squadrons and units including 1st Queens Own Highlanders. On 7th September the ship did another Borneo run before proceeding to Hong Kong for some much needed R&R.

To meet the need for more helicopters in Borneo, RAF aircraft were to be moved from the UK to Libya and *Albion* was despatched to collect them. Arriving in Tobruk on 3rd November she embarked ten Whirlwinds and five Belvederes before returning through the Suez Canal via Aden to the Singapore Straits where the RAF aircraft were launched for shore.

The next stage was to deliver the RAF aircraft to Borneo. With the arrival of these aircraft *Albion* was able to withdraw her own teams who had helped to hold the fort for so long. As well as re-embarking all her own personnel and equipment *Albion* called at Labuan to exchange the 1st KOYLI and the 1st Greenjackets. Albion offloaded the troops in Singapore on 18th December before proceeding to Hong Kong for Christmas, arriving on 23rd December.

Given the lack of accommodation at Labuan a procedure was developed whereby troop rotation via Labuan involved the incoming battalion arriving early in the day, transferring to Whirlwind or Belvedere helicopters and being flown to the various posts being relieved. The troops relieved were flown back to Changi on the same day.

On ANZAC Day in April 1963 Wg/Cdr J.H.R.C. Graves and S/Ldr H.A. Hughes Commanding 3 Squadron RAAF laid wreaths at the Commonwealth Cemetery, accompanied by a party of twenty-three airmen from RAF Butterworth.

1964

January 1964 saw the start of Operation Drogoman, on 3rd January. Five Hastings, four Argosy and two Beverley flew 380 troops to the mainland, four Beverley sorties taking them onward to Tawau. On 5th January there were another six Argosy and three Hastings sorties.

Aircraft attached at that date were:

Whirlwind of 103 & 110 Sqdns   13
Valetta   52   1
Hunters   20   4
Pioneers of RMAF & 209   7
Belvedere   66   2

215 Sqdn Argosy and 34 Sqdn Beverley. (Photo: Boyd)

103 Squadron Whirlwind. (Photo: Boyd)

185

In early 1964 Brian Roche recalls meeting the famous 'Ginger' Lacey, who had served for several years as an aircraft controller. During January Brian Turner watched a Hunter land, realised that it was going too fast, and watched as the undercarriage was retracted; the pilot climbed out before the aircraft stopped and jumped off the wing to safety.

At 03.07 hours on 2nd February a TU 16 Badger overflew at 1000 feet. This happened again on 16th February, this time at 20,000 feet. On 24th February an Air Defence Identification Zone was declared. On the 24th two Javelin FAW 9 fighters of 60 Squadron arrived from Tengah for air defence duties.

60 Squadron Javelin. (Photo: Boyd)

George Middleton, a pilot, was detached to Labuan from Changi RCC/MAROPS to Labuan as Ops Officer. He wrote:

> The Station CO welcomed me and showed me the accommodation earmarked for my operations room, a broom cupboard in the passengers toilets at the airport terminal. I had a W/T operator and a signals pad. Life was simpler in those days.
>
> A Shackleton, usually from 205 Sqdn, was on a rotating detachment at Labuan and was tasked 3 or 4 nights a week to patrol where the Indonesian border met the sea on the east coast of Borneo at Tawau. Infiltrators were thought to sneak around at night in fast patrol boats (FPB) and fishing boats. The Shackletons were supposed to pick them up on radar and identifying them using illuminating flares. The Royal Navy would then dispatch one of its minesweepers to intercept.

186

There were several problems with this scenario. The sea was usually quite calm at night, every floating oil drum, logs and general flotsam registered strongly on the radar. It took great patience and ingenuity to select worthwhile contacts on which to expend the flares, 24 at a time. YEH FPBs and fishing boats (some with 4 blooming great Evinrudes on the stern) were considerably faster than our minesweepers and proved uncatchable. To add spice to the job, every intelligence briefing emphasised that the Indonesians had Mustangs, kindly given to them by our US allies, which would really enjoy some serious shooting practice. It is to the credit to the crews given this job that they accepted it almost without complaint. Only the rations and the transit around the coast, some 360 miles, gave rise to grumbles. If the thunder clouds around the 13,000 ft plus Mount Kinabalu appeared to have subsided by off task time, a dash home across the jungle cut off a considerable corner.

I see from my log book that I got airborne as co-pilot on one of these sorties with Flt Lt Harris in WG 530 on 14 March. I think the regular co-pilot had a cold and a hitherto unfilled ambition to be an Ops Officer in a toilet.

We flew for 9 hours 25 minutes; 5hours day; 4.25 night with .20 minutes actual IF. We took the short cut home and I remember the 20 minutes very well as we skirted Kinabulu in a very bumpy CB. At least I only spent 5 hours thinking about Mustangs.

On 1st March Flight Lieutenant Shields flying Hunter XG 265 of 20 Squadron returned to Labuan with the aircraft on fire. He was forced to eject and subsequently died of his injuries. George Middleton had known Bob Shields from 2nd TAF days: 'He had a problem with one of the drop tanks and returned to Labuan with a very asymmetric fuel load. When he slowed downwind to land, he lost lateral control and had to eject.'

A 45 squadron Canberra WT 209 was detached to Labuan and flew five sorties between 9th and 12th March to calibrate the air defence radar.

George Middleton was summoned to see the Air Commodore in Brunei 'where he had cunningly established his HQ in a girls' school'. George was told that although only a humble Flight Lieutenant he was a valued staff officer and he asked if there were any problems at Labuan. George mentioned the problems of sleeping after night duty in his tent beside the aircraft dispersal. The Air Commodore seemed delighted and promised to sort it out. When George returned he found that his kit had been moved to a proper hut. The only downside was that the Station Commander never

20 Squadron Hunter. (Photo: via B. Roche)

spoke to him again and the mess barman never seemed to serve him until last. At first George shared a room with an air traffic controller who had discovered a profitable hobby; this Polish gentleman collected butterflies, which he then sold at a fair profit. He later shared with a Belvedere helicopter pilot.

A Belvedere helicopter of 66 Squadron had force-landed on a mountain ridge quite high up when one of the two engines had failed. A new engine and a repair party were airlifted in and changed the engine with considerable difficulty; unfortunately during the subsequent ground run some rubbish was ingested and the replacement engine failed. There was no spare in theatre and George's roommate was detailed to make a single engine recovery. George remembered his safe return and thought he had aged visibly. 'He described the operation as a fast taxi to the edge followed by a sickening fall into the abyss. Luckily he managed to gain control while there was still a bit of abyss left.'

In April a Shackleton and Valetta located a lost SAS patrol and dropped food and ammunition to them before their eventual recovery.

Following the move of the Joint Headquarters from Brunei in May there were now ninety officers and 770 other personnel on strength. Brian Roche recalls that following the arrival of an army signals unit under a Major McCready joint high power transmitters were installed to the north of the airfield. Brian also remembers manning the airfield Oerlikons following reports of Mig aircraft buzzing Beverleys over the mainland.

The Airmen's Mess had been built to accommodate 250; with attached personnel there were now over 900 users. St Christopher's Church was

Army Air Corps Beaver. (Photo: Boyd)

completed on 30th May and a dedication service was held on the following day.

There were now a total of thirty-three sleeping huts. The Airport Hotel was taken over as Officers Mess on a two-year lease, with additional hutted officers' accommodation being provided on the Membedai Club site.

William Conway arrived at Labuan in May 1964, working below the ops room as a wireless operator. Time off was spent on the beach, either behind the billets or near the oil terminal. He did a full year tour and remembers enjoying the sing songs in the NAAFI wooden hut.

On 11th June Valetta VW 863 of 52 Squadron returned with a jammed undercarriage and safely belly-landed.

A Mobile Field Photographic Section arrived by Beverley to support two Canberra PR 7s of 58 and 81 Squadrons.

Nigel Graham, an 18-year-old SAC telegraphist, arrived at Labuan in 1964 and worked in the Joint Communication Centre (JCC). He recalls one day being sent, armed with a sten gun, in a mini moke driven by a marine to investigate noise heard at the transmitter station. The staff, uncertain of whether they were being attacked or vandalised, had locked themselves in, and all that Nigel and the marine could see were several recently fallen coconuts; the panic was over. He recalls a motorcycle race, a catamaran and generally enjoying his tour. John Stacey, a SAC engine mechanic worked throughout his tour on the helicopters of 103 and 110 Squadrons.

Peace talks were being held in Tokyo. In preparation for use by UN truce observers helicopters were painted white, with THAILAND marked in blue. The talks failed.

On 21st July Air Marshal Sir Valston Hancock the Chief of Air Staff RAAF visited the station; he had inspected the smaller detachment in 1958 when he was AOC 224 Group.

During July, 27th to 29th, three Indonesian ships, which left Tarakan, were shadowed by a Shackleton as they were considered to be a threat to Tawau. 81 Squadron Canberras flew sorties to observe. Hunter fighters were alerted and on the 28th the ships moved off.

A new Station Commander, Wg Cdr A. Harper AFC, assumed command on 5th August 1964.

Bernard Bale, a Master Navigator on 48 Squadron, returned to Labuan for the first time since 1948 at the end of August; he had last been there with 81 Squadron. He was to visit or stage through en route to Hong Kong on four occasions during the next six weeks. We met in England at our youngest sister's funeral in October and compared notes on how Labuan had expanded in the intervening years.

On 10th September a Whirlwind XJ 760 of 110 Squadron lost power on approach to Long Bangar and force-landed in the jungle. On the following day a Twin Pioneer XP 294 of 209 Squadron skidded on landing at Bario into a ditch, an undercarriage leg collapsed and the aircraft sustained Cat 5 damage.

During September Doug Allen, who had first served at Labuan in 1954 while flying Mosquito PR34 with 81 Squadron, was detached from Changi to Labuan as an aircraft captain of 215 Squadron. He had converted to the AW Argosy and flown out from the UK when the squadron moved to Changi. Having previously trained pilots on Oxford aircraft during the war and flown Hastings, Mosquito, Hornet and Canberra aircraft Doug was not generally impressed with the Argosy, criticising the altitude capability in particular. One notable thing he does remember is that the seats were very good!

His aircraft during this detachment was Argosy XR 108 and his co-pilot Fg Off Paice The allotted tasks for his detached duty was to drop a series of one-ton containers to jungle sites, a task that required accurate flying and a careful getaway. These included Pasia, Bario, Pensiangan, and Long Jiwi. He allowed a co-pilot to carry out one drop, but found that the young man was so delighted with his approach and drop that he very nearly left it too late to pull out over a nearby hill.

In *Ballykelly Shackleton Era (1952–1971)* David Hill wrote:

A Coastal Command detachment was to be sent to bolster 205 Squadron, the resident Shackleton squadron at Changi, Singapore. The

210 Squadron Shackleton. (Photo: Boyd)

task fell to the Ballykelly squadrons, and as the duration of the commitment was obviously uncertain it was planned that each squadron
would in turn nominally take command of the four aircraft/ four crew
detachment for a three month period. Crews and aircraft could,
however, be drawn from all three squadrons at any time during the
detachment. No.204 Sqn. took control of the first phase of the
detachment, which left Ballykelly on 11 September.

The Shackleton's role during Confrontation was to fly patrols
(codenamed Hawk Moth) out over the Straits of Malacca to try to
detect clandestine infiltrations of the Malaysian coast by the Indonesians. A sub-detachment of two aircraft was also set up at Labuan,
aircraft and crews rotating every two weeks. The patrols turned out to
be mostly routine with the odd exciting moment now and again. No.
203 Sqn. took over the detachment from 210 followed by 204 and this
was the pattern of events until the commitment, as far as the Ballykelly
squadrons were concerned, ended with the completion of 204's second
stint in January 1966.

David Price an ex-rigger also recalls:

During my time on 205 squadron, 1965–67 there was a permanent
detachment at Labuan of two Shackletons, two aircrews and the
ground crew all doing two weeks at a time. From the ground crew
point of view it was a piece of cake one aircraft flew each night, as a
result most of the memories are of the social side. The flights were to

Kuching or Tawau on alternate nights I don't suppose anybody on the other side could have worked out the pattern. Prior to one trip up to Lab I remember assisting in collecting all Changi store's stock of portable oxygen bottles, the Shackleton didn't have a permanent oxygen system, only portable oxygen bottles under each seat, I think 10 minutes duration. It had been decided that Kuching/Tawau could be done in one night with an overland transit but of course there were some hills in the way. I can recall that the galley bunks were covered with these additional portable oxygen bottles.

Flt Lt J. Firth, flying a Pioneer of 209 Squadron lost power and landed on a road, recovered and flew the aircraft back to base and was recommended for a Green Endorsement.

In September the Borneo Airways hangar was taken over as a servicing bay.

In late October five Canberras of 14 Squadron RNZAF were attached to fly low-level sorties over Sabah.

At the end of December Flt Lt Rickards' 45 Squadron Canberra crew were detached from Tengah to carry out border patrols, in order to reduce the demands made on shorter range Javelin and Hunter aircraft.

During this month a Comet of 51 Squadron stayed one night leaving on the following day on a Sigint flight down the eastern coast of Indonesian Borneo, landing in Darwin.

During 1964 there were seven fatalities airlifted to Singapore and over 250 Casevac cases of all categories. 129 Signals Unit reported a total of over 46,000 aircraft arrivals and eleven scrambles against reported bogeys, five diversions from patrol against bogeys and three to escort aircraft in distress back to Labuan.

1965

It became practice in early 1965 for 45 Squadron Canberra to be more or less permanently based at Labuan, five crews rotating through Labuan during that month, this practice continuing for another two months.

'Rusty' Blagden, an SAC telegraphist, had married in November 1964 and two months later arrived at Labuan, after a brief hectic spell at RAF Changi, for a one year unaccompanied tour. Once he had a found a bed space he started work in the Joint Communications Centre (JCC); although 'Joint' it was in fact run by the army.

The JCC was established at Labuan in January 1965. Rusty worked alongside 266 Signals Section with a few Royal Navy staff nearby. Security was very tight and safe disposal, by incineration, of redundant paperwork at the end of a shift was diligently carried out.

Rusty described a small tent not far from the compound entrance and here lived an Indian local, affectionately named 'Pop'. He had an old camp bed and a couple of boxes, set on duckboards were his primus cooker, foodstuff and newspaper with which he would wrap the egg and bacon 'banjo'. Although breakfast in the mess was acceptable, Rusty reckoned that an egg and bacon banjo from Pop was tops along with his teas, coffees and humour. A couple of his famous phrases were 'drop a bollock' and 'think you are on Daddie's yacht'. Rusty still wonders what might have happened to him when JCC closed.

Rusty remembers a very good CSE show given by Acker Bilk, and visiting the new NAAFI and cinema. For Christmas 1965 there was promise of turkey for lunch, but somebody broke into the mess and stole all three; suspicion fell on the RAAF ground crew of the Sabre detachment, but it was never proved.

During a battle between Ghurka forces and 90 Indonesians on 12th February near Longbang, Javelins flew low afterburner runs and drove the Indonesian forces back across the border.

Flight Lieutenant Perry flying Whirlwind XD 183 of 110 Squadron suffered the loss of the tip of his tail rotor on 27th January; he made a forced landing and slept in the helicopter overnight. Ground crew changed the tail pylon, tail drive shaft, the rotor gearbox and rotor assembly; despite the lack of instruments the helicopter was flown back to base.

In March twelve Whirlwind 10s of 230 Squadron arrived aboard HMS *Bulwark* following their long move from Germany and were flown ashore. 230 had operated Whirlwind HAR 10 helicopters since 1962; with their Bristol Siddeley Gnome turboshaft propulsion they were considered ideal for the hot high area of operations. The squadron had flown from Gutersloh to Odiham to prepare for service in Borneo; armoured pilot's seats were fitted and Bren gun mountings for the doorways.

Nine Whirlwinds were embarked in HMS *Triumph*, four more collected in Cyprus. The squadron air and ground crews flew by charter aircraft. After local training the complete unit embarked in HMS *Bulwark* for Labuan in March 1965 arriving on 10th March. Operations began the same day, the CO taking Maj Gen W.C. Walker CBE DSO to Muara. The squadron established a detachment at Tawau, the main task being re-supply and reinforcement of forward patrols along a 120-mile sector of frontier. The first units supported were 42 Commando RM and 2/7 Ghurkhas.

In April 1965 Flight Lieutenant McEachern in XP 396 and Sergeant G. Ashall, crewman rescued two civilians, landing on a ridge on Mount Kinabulu at 8300 feet and waiting nine hours for the injured to be brought 5000 feet down from the peak.

During the first full month 200 sorties were flown, and the CO expressed himself very satisfied with the squadron's achievement. Difficulties arose later due to Labuan being at the end of a very long supply line and some doubts were expressed as to whether Command were aware of the spares situation.

The squadron carried a medical team to immunise local village children and also extracted Australian SAS patrols.

During April a Javelin radar caught fire, followed by another Javelin starter blowing up; both aircraft were saved from further damage.

At the end of April 45 Squadron were required to leave Tengah to allow runway repairs. Six aircraft made the move to Labuan. One of them was WT 206, a Canberra B 6 that was needed for a special task.

An Air Weapons Range had been laid out and supervised at Balambangan Island, off the northernmost tip of Sabah. This island had been one of the first British trading posts in the area; it had been set up in 1761 by the British East India Company as a free port for trade with China, although it was never successful and was abandoned. The island was licensed for use as a range; 45 Squadron weapons training was carried out as well as the border patrols. In June most of the 45 Squadron aircraft returned to Tengah leaving one available for operations from Labuan.

Nigel Woodger wrote on the RAF Forum:

I had been in the RAF only 11 months when I got my posting to 129 Signals Unit, Labuan. Originally due to report to Brize Norton but then flew from Heathrow by BOAC VC10 via Beirut and Bombay.

At Changi I spent a great week in Singapore before the F/Sgt caught me, declaring I would be on the 07.30 flight.

Nigel overslept, arrived late and found that the original Hastings had taxied to the end of the runway, and returned with an engine problem.

Half an hour later we boarded the plane and taxied to the end of the runway, engines were revved up and then suddenly one belched thick black smoke so back we went to departure. After another half hour we were put on an RAF coach to be taken to Changi Creek Hotel for some breakfast. Finally getting airborne we arrived at Labuan. The plane landed and then stopped on the runway, where we were all ordered off to walk to the arrival hall.

The aircraft had been immediately grounded on landing as another Hastings had crashed near Abingdon on 6th July killing all 41 on board. That was my arrival in Labuan my home for the next 12 months. The Hastings were grounded following this accident for inspection and rectification of the elevator hinge bolt bracket and 48 Squadron did not resume flying until September.

I didn't realise anywhere could be as hot as this, the old coarse KD rubbing places I didn't even realise I had. After picking up my bedding, two sheets one blanket and a mozzie net, I got a lift in a Land Rover down to my billet. S'truth it's made out of corrugated iron. The billet was 100 ft long, which included a 10-foot veranda at each end, inside there were 10 beds down each side along with a small locker and the usual one door wardrobe. Thankfully there were three large electric fans supported from the ceiling all of which were going full pelt from the day I arrived to the day I left.

Toilet facilities consisted of another long corrugated building; at one end were six showers (six pipes with a stop tap on each), these functioned for a short time each day due to water shortage. Many is the person who got lathered up to have the water stop before they could rinse off, nasty in the heat there as it could cause a condition called 'tinia'. Next to the showers were two troughs on stilts with about four taps to each washbasin. No hot water again same as showers unless you happened to go in when the sun had been shining on the pipes during the afternoon. The rest of this building was a row of about 10 toilets, yes just the toilets no dividing walls or doors (walls and doors were added in 1966.)

The Mess hall was a similar building to the accommodation; the rough table tops were three planks of wood with a healthy gap between them. When you took your food to a table and set it down, it was a race between you and the cockroaches.

Some complained about Labuan, I was there for a year and would have stayed longer if I had had the chance, there was never a dull moment. When I got there the Naafi comprised two old marquees joined down their long sides, we had a cinema next to the mess hall (bring your own mozzie coils), which attracted all sorts of wonderful flying nightlife. Membedai beach was only two minutes walk from the billet, Crocodile Beach just a bit further north, named after the sea crocs that lived there. If you wanted a longer walk, about a mile, there was Shell Beach and Club that had sailing boats, a power boat and water skis and it was only a five minute walk from there into the town of Victoria, which had numerous pubs, eating-places, a cinema, and an air-conditioned hotel with live entertainment.

In July Whirlwind helicopter XP 402 of 230 Squadron was lost, while hovering at low level while taking part in a display at a Labuan Red Cross fete; it suffered complete engine failure and crashed in the sea, injuring the three crew members.

In the first year the squadron had flown 5742 hours and had carried over two million pounds of freight, 25,539 passengers and 295 casualties. .

By the middle of 1965 Labuan was a crowded and extremely busy Station. Movements that had been fewer than 100 a month prior to Confrontation had by now risen to over 2500 per month.

129 Signals Unit scrambled aircraft on 8th September following border violations by an Indonesian B26 and two Mustangs and later on the 16th, dealt with two live bogies, following a delayed report of intrusion by an Indonesian MIG 17 (Fresco) and a C130 Hercules; the latter was forced down and crashed in Indonesian territory.

Wing Commander D.L. Pinn assumed command in 1965. The officer establishment comprised a senior M O, a Sqn ldr O C admin, a catering officer, three secretarial, three education, two equipment, eight operations and an intelligence officer. There were three engineers, one ground support, one electronic and a radar specialist as well as nine air traffic control officers and a chaplain.

Valetta crews were a Master Pilot, a Master Navigator, a F/Sgt air signaller and a F/Sgt AQM. The Pembroke crew comprised a Master Pilot and a Master Navigator. Airman strength totalled twelve warrant officers, 101 senior NCOs and 490 airmen.

Gerald Law wrote in 2007:

I was only at Labuan for a fortnight. I was on 20 Squadron based at Tengah in 1965. We flew Hunter FGA9's and had Forward Elements at Kuching and Labuan. Owing to an increase in activity, we sent 2 additional aircraft with myself, an Engines and an Airframes bloke. After 2 weeks the trouble eased off and I returned to Tengah. The only memorable thing to happen was a cholera scare, which meant that there was no ice available for drinks in the NAAFI. It was interesting to stroll along the beach, as there were bits of aircraft engines sticking out of the sand. Apparently they were what remained of Japanese aircraft that didn't make the runway. There was also a rotting landing craft on the beach.

Early in October the 64 Squadron detachment of Javelins left to be replaced by Hunters of 20 Squadron. The Hunters in turn were relieved by RAAF Sabres of 77 Squadron. This squadron, then equipped with P40 Kittyhawks, had been one of the first to arrive after the liberation of the island, equipped with the Sabre they had staged through Labuan in 1959.

The last 45 Squadron Canberra detachment returned to Tengah in November but the squadron carried out bombing practice at Balambangan using 1000-pound bombs during December, continuing into the new year, flying from Tengah and refuelling at Labuan before flying back to Tengah.

77 Squadron RAAF were relieved by 3 Squadron RAAF, also equipped with CAC Sabres, from Butterworth during November and remained until after Christmas.

Paul Thompson, an SAC assistant air traffic controller, arrived from Kai Tak via Changi, just before Christmas 1965 and worked in the ComAirBor Ops room. Briefly left alone during celebrations, he answered a phone call from 3 Squadron RAAF on QRA asking if they could investigate approaching aircraft; he gave the OK and off they went to the eventual horror of everybody further up the chain of command. The Sabres found a mere flock of birds and beat up the airfield on their return, which was the first time the top brass knew they were airborne. Paul could have used the old excuse, 'It seemed like a good idea at the time.'

During 1965 there were 298 casualties evacuated to Singapore.

1966

In January 1966 aircraft strength comprised a Pembroke WV 725 and Valettas XV 524 and WJ 498. No 230 Squadron were operating eleven Westland Whirlwind helicopters, together with the six Whirlwinds of 848 Squadron Royal Navy. There were two Beverleys attached from No 34 Squadron, Canberras of 45 Squadron, and seven Hunters of 20 Squadron. There were six Twin Pioneers, two of 209 Squadron and four of the Royal Malaysian Air Force (RMAF). The lone Shackleton carried out fourteen sorties during the month.

A 45 Squadron Canberra XK 641 crewed by Fg Off Barnes, Flt Lt Perrin and Fg Off Stevenson were detached to Labuan to carry out border patrols and Forward Air Controller (FAC) training at the end of January. Ted Heath MBE MP the Leader of the Opposition visited the Station that month.

In February the Shackleton was diverted to assist the ship *Ho Sang* aground on Friedrich reef. HMNZS ship *Taranaki* was sent to assist the freighter, which subsequently refloated and proceeded on its journey.

The Chief of Air Staff Air Chief Marshal Sir Charles Elworthy GCB, CBE, DSO, MVO, DFC, MA paid an official visit on 15th March.

In April 1966 a Beverley carried out a successful drop of a Caterpillar D4 bulldozer in to a DZ, the bulldozer operating within twenty minutes of air delivery. Later in the month the town Avgas bulk supply was found to be contaminated, leaving the airfield with only 14,000 gallons, including barrelled stocks. Until the matter was rectified aircraft were routed via Brunei or Jesselton. On the last trip of each day Beverley aircraft uplifted fuel from the mainland and transferred to bowsers. When the town tanks had been cleaned and replenished the airfield still had 10,000 gallons.

On 15th May Canberras of 45 Squadron dropped six 1000 pounders in the Central Brigade area and the following day two aircraft dropped more bombs in Eastern Brigade's area.

Mike Durrant, who normally worked in Station Workshops, joined the Labuan Broadcasting Service (LBS), which was run as a club; members paid a subscription for the privilege of broadcasting to the station. When he joined, most of the membership worked at 129 SU; they were the founders who had set it up. LBS was a rediffusion system, which was broadcast down a network of wires to loudspeakers in all the domestic accommodation. The standard was such that the BBC allowed us to broadcast recorded transcriptions of their programmes, a facility not normally granted. Most programmes were in fact 'home made', including the sound effects for plays and shows. The 'Top 20' was broadcast live twice a week, to keep people up to date. One of the highlights was relaying the BBC live broadcast of the World Cup when England beat Germany, when a late night was enjoyed by all.

Mike became Senior Controller and took over as Chief Engineer when Derek Warner of 129 SU returned to UK at the end of his tour. The biggest engineering problem was preventing the station radio 'ham' breaking through with his ground wave and interfering with the broadcast; more hazardous was repairing or installing cables to the huts – it was found that most of the corrugated iron roofs were live at mains voltage.

Mike saved his leave and money to buy a house on return to the UK and remembers celebrating his birthday in a bar in Victoria with Maori singing him a Maori birthday greeting.

During May and June Mike Spence and Jack Newberry ferried a De Haviland Heron from the UK to Hawaii, night stopping at Labuan at the end of the month. They found a very busy base, 'with an air of efficiency, enthusiasm and high morale', after 'being marshalled to a very crowded parking area'.

In May 1966, 5 Squadron RMAF arrived to assemble and train with their new Alluoette SA 316 helicopters. A month later D Flight of 848 Squadron Royal Navy departed aboard HMS *Albion*.

The NAAFI Town Club was opened on 13th June by the Director of Borneo Operations, Major General G.H. Lea CB, DSO, MBE.

On 16th July Wg Cdr L.W. Phipps AFC assumed command of the Station. On the 26th the AOC 224 Group presented the Station Badge, which after a few changes by the Heralds, had been officially authorised by Defence Council Instruction T 311 on 20th July 1966.

On 11th August 1966 Indonesia and Malaysia approved the ratification of the peace agreement that had been negotiated at Bangkok earlier in the year. This announcement marked the formal end of the confrontation between the two countries. RAF presence was gradually reduced in the following months. During August the Shackleton of 205 Squadron returned to Changi, and there were no further maritime or fighter detachments.

45 Squadron Canberras had now been modified to enable use of the French Nord AS 30 missile and in August deployed to Labuan to fire twenty of these missiles on the Balambangan range.

Wing Commander Phipps observed that, although in theory this meant cessation of hostilities, in fact full-scale operations were continuing in the interior, directed against a strong band of Indonesian regulars who had crossed into Sarawak and were headed for Brunei. The Station was fully engaged with transport operations in support of British forces.

The pace of activity gradually slackened during August, and plans were made during this time for the commitment to act as the main airhead for the withdrawal of British and Commonwealth troops from East Malaysia during the following two months. Plans were also made for despatching equipment and the future reduction of personnel numbers. During October there were as many as fifty resident aircraft involved in replacing British and Commonwealth troops with Malaysian forces

By the end of August 1966 230 Squadron Whirlwind helicopters were returned to the UK aboard five Short Belfast aircraft lifts. The final figures for the squadron in Borneo were 8,558 hours, over three millions pounds of freight, 3,779 passengers and 414 casualties carried.

110 Squadron arrived from Kuching with ten Whirlwinds. John Lockett, an airframe tech, had been with the squadron since July and did as many trips as possible to assist the loadmaster. One memorable flight was to

230 Sqdn helicopters loading into Belfast. (Photo: John Gilbert via B. Roche)

accompany Wg Cdr Flying, who had obtained permission to fly two circuits of the Brunei mosque.

The primary task for the future role of RAF Labuan was to support the developing Royal Malaysian Air Force strength. The RAF would continue to run the airfield services of air traffic control, operations, and fire services at Labuan, and provide air transport support for the Malaysian forces with six Whirlwind Mk 10 helicopters. The aircraft would come from RAF Seletar, the pilots from 110 Squadron; the ground crew would be Labuan personnel. In addition the intention was to continue as a staging post for RAF aircraft within the theatre, and if necessary for aircraft on the westbound route from the UK to Singapore. It was also likely to be used for occasional training exercises within the Command.

On 9th October 845 Squadron helicopters flew aboard HMS *Bulwark*, the last Royal Navy participation in the Confrontation campaign.

The two Valetta aircraft left for RAF Seletar in November. On 27th December the last 48 Squadron Hastings left for RAF Changi, making a low pass in farewell.

By this time the unit strength had been reduced to 280 personnel. Christmas dinner was served in the Sergeants Mess to the few remaining, forty or so, airmen and a couple of soldiers.

Royal Malaysian Air Force (RMAF) presence was varied. Caribou of No 1 Squadron left for Kuala Lumpur and were replaced by 8 Squadron.

RMAF Twin Pioneer. (Photo: Boyd)

RMAF Handley Page Herald. (Photo: Boyd)

RMAF D H C Caribou. (Photo: Boyd)

1967

January 1967 saw the first visit to Labuan of a Hawker Siddeley Andover of 52 Squadron. Following the realisation that the RMAF would have to bear full costs of the unit it was decided that 110 Squadron helicopters would return to Singapore. The revised strength would be twelve Officers and 100 airmen.

In February a 66 Squadron Belvedere helicopter flew from Kuching to lift out an engine from a RMAF Caribou that had crashed and return it to Labuan.

In March Sqn Ldr D.H. Wood assumed command; the unit would revert to becoming a staging post with an intended strength of one officer and thirty airmen.

During August a Shackleton of 205 Squadron set off on an eastabout exercise from Changi, returned to Changi u/s, staged through Labuan, once again returned u/s, was rectified and then flew onward to Guam.

In September Sqn Ldr E.W.J. Morris assumed command; the unit by now comprised four officers; fourteen senior NCOs and sixty airmen. By November this had been reduced to four officers, twelve SNCOs and forty-four airmen.

1968

In February 1968 Flying Officer P.L. Wood assumed command; the Detachment was once again to be parented by RAF Changi. A major hiccup was caused by a delay of six days in paying the airmen.

On 5th February LCT *Ardennes* docked to return surplus stores and MT vehicles to Singapore. During March the fire vehicles and refuellers were transferred to RMAF. Landing Ship *Sir Bedevere* docked on 25th March for further equipment return to Singapore.

A party of ten suppliers under the leadership of F/O Martin flew in by Andover for a one-month detachment in early 1968, living in the Victoria Hotel. The main purpose was to take stock of the Labuan inventories prior to its closure.

One of the party liked the beautiful beaches, but found 'the weather was hotter than Singapore. The only break in the monotony was the drone of aircraft engines from the RMAF Caribou squadron in training. Frustration grew each time an Andover landed; I was not on the list to return. Finally time to return - no, not on an Andover but by sea on board *Sir Galahad*, reaching Singapore after 4 days at sea.'

On 18th April Sqn Ldr W.R. Roberts relieved F/O Wood for the final run down, by which time there were five SNCOs and twenty-four airmen remaining.

The Labuan Broadcasting Service closed on 14th May and the cinema on the 31st. On 9th June there was a farewell barbecue at the Sabah Marine Club. Labuan Town Board invited all to a farewell party in the Civic Centre on 15th June, but this had to be declined because by that date all RAF personnel had left.

Thus ended more than twenty years of Royal Air Force presence at Labuan.

Over the years RAF aircraft have passed through Labuan. One on record is during July 1969; three Shackleton aircraft WL 758, W and WL 748 R landed at Labuan en route Singapore on a west about route from Guam.

David Ketcher, a photographer, did a detachment to Labuan with 81 Squadron in 1969 to complete the Borneo survey which had been ongoing since World War II. His duties were to annotate all the negative film with titles and number each frame, which was a lot with 6 × F52 cameras each with 500 feet of film! There was an Indonesian liaison officer present all the time to check the coverage. The RAF had left the base by then and it was owned by the RMAF (Malaysian Air Force).

Epilogue

Following the successful conclusion of the Confrontation campaign and the British government decision to withdraw from East of Suez, the RAF rarely visited Labuan. The island became part of Sabah following the establishment of Malaysia in 1963, and in 1984 Labuan was ceded to the federal government by Sabah and became a federal territory. In 1990 it was declared an international offshore financial centre and free trade zone.

We visited in December 2009 and were surprised to see how many ships were laid up in Brunei Bay. We considered that a Sunderland pilot would have found great difficulty in finding a suitable alighting area. However, it was good to see how the island had developed in the interim years yet still preserved the memory and commemorated those men for whom Labuan was their last resting place.

Appendix

Commanding Officers RAF Labuan

1945	
December	Gp Capt F.C. Sturgiss OBE
1946	S/Ldr K.W. Nicholson, 230 Sqdn Detachment
January 12th	Flt Lt S H Kingaby, 104 Embarkation Unit
May–June	Fg Off Challoner, 104 Emb Unit disbanded
1948	Flt Lt Scott, OC Detachment
1949	Flt Lt H.E. Gundry
1950	Fg Off G. Meyrick
1955	Flt Lt J. Duncombe AFC
1956	Flt Lt J.B. Knight
1957	Flt Lt D.J. Dunnachie
1957	Flt Lt D.H. Morley
1958	Flt Lt J. Atkinson
1958	Flt Lt M Fleetwood
1961	Flt Lt M J W Pierson
1962	Flt Lt D Borrett
December	Wg Cdr T.R.C.H. Graves, OC Detachment
1963	Station Commander
August	Wg Cdr W.E. Thomas AFC Station Commander
1964 August	Wg Cdr A. Harper AFC
1965	Wg Cdr D.L. Pinn MBE
1966 July	Wg Cdr L.W. Phipps AFC
1967 March	Sqn Ldr D.H. Wood
Unit reverted to Staging Post	
September	Sqn Ldr E.W.J. Morris
1968 February	Fg Off P.L. Wood
April	Sqn Ldr W.R. Roberts for Final Rundown

Printed Sources

HANSARD
1. *The Battle for Miri, Sarawak, Borneo* by Franz L Kessler (authorsden.com) has compiled pieces from the Internet and other sources about the invasion. The Japanese needed the Seria and Miri oilfields, and the Lutong refinery.
2. RAF FORUM website
3. No 230 Sqdn *Fly Past* December 2006 Guy Warner pp. 102–106 (Roger Wain, Tony Wickes
4. British Official History; *The War Against Japan Volume1 The Loss of Singapore* (Chapter XIII) by Major General S. Woodburn Kirby
5. *Three Came Home*, Agnes Keith
6. *SANDAKAN A Conspiracy of Silence*, Lynette Ramsay Silver. Milner 1998. Reproduced by permission.
    AIR WAR AGAINST JAPAN: Australian War Memorial (A.W.M. 1968) George Odgers
    pacificwrecks.com/provinces/borneo-labuan recorded American Missions against Labuan from December 1944–June 18 1945
    Journal: Dr OOI KEAT GIN A.W.M.
    The World at War Australian tank deployment Graham Donaldson /worldatwar.net/article/australiantank/brunei45
    Always First: Airfield Construction Squadrons RAAF David Wilson
    Silas Edwards 4 Airfield Construction Squadron. (ACS) (AWM)
    Don Northmore 5 A C S (AWM)
    Secrets Revealed No. 3 Squadron RAAF 1916–1991
    Peter Muller and John Hutchison
    An Illustrated History of 77 Squadron RAAF 1942–1992 Swift to Destroy. ISBN 0 642 16999 3. Reproduced by permission.
    The Flying Camels: The History of 45 Squadron RAF, Jeff Jefford
7. *Eastward: A History of the Royal Air Force in the FAR EAST 1945–1972* A C M Sir David Lee HMSO Books
    HMS *Albion* World Cruise brochure 1958–1959
    FLASHBACK of the Roman Catholic Church Labuan (1857–1998)
    BALLYKELLY: Shackleton Era (1952–1971) David Hill
    HUNT LIKE a TIGER The History of 230 Squadron 1939–45, Tom Docherty Woodfield

Useful Reading

A Gust of Plumes, Darrell Bates, Hodder and Stoughton 1972
Confrontation 1962–66, Nick van der Bijl, Pen and Sword
Conflict and Confrontation in S.E. Asia 1961–1965, Matthew Jones, published
   by Cardiff University Press 2001
Bristol Beaufighter, Jerry Scutts, Crowood Aviation Series 2004, The Crowood
   Press Ltd, Ramsbury, Marlborough, Wilts SN8 2HR
Drop Zone Borneo, Roger Annett, Pen and Sword

National Archive References

Admiralty

ADM 53/ 148278	HMS *Albion* LOG 1958

Air

AIR20/10373	Loss of VP254. 1958–1959
AIR20/10374	Loss of VP254. 1959–1960
AIR 23/2386	Organisation RAF Borneo
AIR27/ Series	Squadron Operational Record Books
AIR 28/ Series	Station Operational Record Books
AIR 29/ Series	Unit Operational Record Books
AIR 49/ 112	300 Group Operational Record

Colonial Office

CO 537/915	Japancsc land purchase 1923
CO 874/378	Naval, military resources 1931–38
CO 874/379	Naval, military resources 1939–42
CO 937/266	Airport 1952–54

War Office

WO 172/ 95	Punjab Regiment 1941
WO 172/213	Punjab Regiment 1941
WO 32/11166	Military Administration BNB 1944–46
WO 172/10044	Civil Affairs Unit B Borneo 1946

Acknowledgements

The author wishes to thank the following for their help:
American Battle Monuments Commission
Australian War Memorial
Commonwealth War Graves Commission
Public Record Office/National Archives, Kew

Australia: ADF Serials team; Gordon Birkett, Gordon Clarke, Brendan Cowan, Grahame Higgs, Jan Herivel, Ron Wynn, and the rest of the ADF Serials Team. AVM F.W. Barnes, Frank A. Lees, Tony Miles, Lynette Ramsay Silver, Jim Treadwell, Tom Wilson, Vic Wise.
Brunei: David Wilson.
Cyprus: Rusty Blagden.
Labuan: Willie Teo.
New Zealand: Cess Crooks.
Philippines: Brian Turner.
UK: Doug Allen, Reginald Allen, the late Ken Appleford, Phyll Bale for her proof reading and support, Bruce Blanche, A. Boyd, W. Brown, Ian Carr, Peter Charles, W. Conway, Vic Dabin, Jack Dent, J. Dyer, Ken Dix, M. Durrant, John Feltham, Basil Frost, J. Gilbert, N. Graham, E. Heywood, Bill Hyland, David Ketcher, Jeff Jefford, Bill Kelley, John Lambert, John Lockett, Brian Lowans, A. McDougall, Ivor Orton, R. Preston, D. Price, the late E. Pursglove, B. Roche, J. Sawyer, K. Shaw, M. Snowling, Reg Solway, Nigel Springthorpe, J. Stacey, Paul Trotter, and the late Tony Wilson.

Index

211